Showing Up for Life

Thoughts on the Gifts of a Lifetime

BILL GATES SR.

with Mary Ann Mackin

BROADWAY BOOKS

NEW YORK

Published in the United States by Broadway Books, an imprint
of The Crown Publishing Group, a division of Random
House, Inc., New York.
www.broadwaybusinessbooks.com

Broadway Books and its logo, a letter B bisected on the
diagonal, are trademarks of Random House, Inc.

LIBRARY OF CONGRESS CATALOGING-IN-PUBLICATION DATA
Gates, William H.
Showing up for life : thoughts on the gifts of a lifetime /
Bill Gates Sr. with Mary Ann Mackin. – 1st ed.
p. cm.
1. Voluntarism. 2. Problem solving. 3. Generosity. I. Mackin,
Mary Ann. II. Title.
HN49.V64G38 2009
179'.9—dc22
2008050080
[B]

ISBN 978-0-385-52701-9

PRINTED IN THE UNITED STATES OF AMERICA

1 3 5 7 9 10 8 6 4 2

First Edition

This book is dedicated to all the

World-Class Shower Uppers I've met in my life

who continue to inspire me.

Contents

Showing Up for Life

FOREWORD

Dad, the next time somebody asks you if you're the real Bill Gates, I hope you say, "Yes." I hope you tell them that you're all the things the other one strives to be.

–Bill Gates

Some Second Thoughts About Thinking

In the early days of Microsoft's success, when my son's name was starting to become known to the world at large, everybody from reporters at *Fortune* magazine to the checkout person at the local grocery store would ask me, "How do you raise a kid like that? What's the secret?"

At those moments I was generally thinking to myself, "Oh, it's a secret all right . . . because I don't get it either!"

My son, Bill, has always been known in our family as Trey.

When we were awaiting his arrival, knowing that if the baby was a boy he would be named "Bill Gates III," his maternal grandmother and great-grandmother thought of the confusion that would result from having two Bills in the same household. Inveterate card players, they suggested we call him "Trey," which, as any card player knows, refers to the number three card.

As a young boy, Trey probably read more than many other kids and he often surprised us with his ideas about how he thought the world worked. Or imagined it could work.

Like other kids his age, he was interested in science fiction. He was curious and thoughtful about things adults had learned to take for granted or were just too busy to think about.

His mother, Mary, and I often joked about the fact that Trey sometimes moved slowly and was often late.

It seemed like every time we were getting ready to go somewhere everybody else in the family would be out in the car—or at least have their coats on. And then someone would ask, "Where's Trey?"

Someone else would reply, "In his room."

Trey's room was in our daylight basement, a partially above-ground area with a door and windows looking out on the yard. So his mother would call down to him, "Trey, what are you doing down there?"

Once Trey shot back, "I'm thinking, mother. Don't *you* ever think?"

Imagine yourself in our place. I was in the most demanding years of my law practice. I was a dad, a husband, doing all the things parents in families do. My wife, Mary, was raising three kids, volunteering for the United

Way, and doing a million other things. And your child asks you if you ever take time to think.

Mary and I paused and looked at each other. And then we answered in unison, "No!"

However, now that I've had nearly half a century to reflect on my son's question, I'd like to change my answer to it.

Yes I think. I think about many things.

For example, reflecting on my own experience raising a family, I think about how as parents most of us try to feel our way through the challenges that come with being married and raising children. We have very little formal training for those roles, and they are two of the most difficult and important things we'll ever undertake.

I think about the inequities that exist in our world and about the opportunities we have to correct them, opportunities that have never existed before in all of human history.

I also think about less critical concerns, such as when the University of Washington Huskies might make it to the Rose Bowl.

Lately, I've been wondering if any of that thinking is worth passing on to others.

I realize that I have been privileged to meet many remarkable people whose stories might be inspiring or helpful to other people.

Also, in reflecting on our family's life when our children were young, it has occurred to me that our experiences might be useful or at least interesting to other families.

There is one lesson I've learned over the years as a father, lawyer, activist, and citizen which stands above all the others that I hope to convey in these pages. It is simply this: We are all in this life together and we need each other.

Showing Up for Life

Eighty percent of success is showing up.
—Woody Allen, from *Love & Death*

A few years ago I received an award from the YMCA.

The day the award was to be presented I looked around the crowded ballroom wondering why all those people were making such a fuss over me.

The only thing I could come up with was that I show up a lot.

When I was a young lawyer in the 1950s, I first became involved with causes in the community by joining the board of the YMCA, where I had spent many happy hours as a college student.

After a while, I decided I wanted to do more to show up in my community and help out in a hands-on way.

So along with doing pro bono law work, I started serving on committees and boards for everything from the chamber of commerce to school levy campaigns. Over time the nature of some of them changed and the number grew. At the same time my wife, Mary, was showing up for her own list of causes.

Why do I show up so much? Well, I suppose there are a lot of reasons.

I show up because I care about a cause. Or because I care about the person who asked me to show up. And maybe sometimes I show up because it irritates me when other people *don't* show up.

My obsessive showing up has become a joke among my children. Still, I notice they've picked up the habit. And frankly, that's what happened to me.

I started showing up because as far back as I can remember I watched other people I admired showing up.

In my hometown of Bremerton, Washington, showing up to lend your neighbors a hand was just something decent people did. My parents, on a scale of one to ten, were nines at showing up. My dad was somebody people knew they could count on. If there was money to be raised for a good cause, my dad was always willing to call on people and ask them to give a few dollars. He had led the effort to have a new park built in town. I read about it in an old newspaper long after he died. I had not known about it, but it didn't surprise me.

My mom showed up for a long list of community activities that included everything from picnics to fund drives.

My parents never talked about showing up. They just did it.

Another adult who provided me with powerful life lessons in showing up was our next-door neighbor, Dorm Braman. He showed up for so many things and accomplished so much in his life you'd have thought it would take two men to live Dorm's life.

Dorm owned a cabinet-making business and in his spare time he led our Boy Scout troop.

He was a remarkable man whose showing up touched a lot of lives. In fact, even though he had never graduated from high school, after we Boy Scouts were all in college, Dorm ran for mayor of Seattle and won. Later, he was appointed by President Richard Nixon as assistant secretary of transportation.

In the early years when he was our Scoutmaster, one weekend every month—rain or shine—Dorm took us on adventures that ranged from laid-back camping trips to arduous twenty-mile hikes through the Olympic Mountains.

One year he even acquired an old bus, added more seats to it, and took all of us to Yellowstone and Glacier national parks.

Far and away the most unforgettable memory I have of Dorm's showing up involved the building of what we called Camp Tahuya and Sundown Lodge.

This adventure began when Dorm decided our Boy

Scout troop was going to acquire its own campsite and on it build a marvelous log lodge.

The first step was to persuade the local Lions Club to back the idea and buy the troop the land. We named the place Camp Tahuya after the river that ran through it.

Once we had the site, Dorm taught us how to clear land, fell trees, and build.

A lot has changed since then.

At that time, we felled the trees by hand and sawed the logs into proper lengths using two-man crosscut saws,

Building a log lodge is sweaty, gritty work. But this adventure proved to us that if we worked together long enough and hard enough anything was possible. *Photo, 1938.*

and hand-peeled and planed them smooth and to proper dimensions using hand-wielded adzes. We had one power tool—a circular saw powered by Dorm's flatbed truck.

Every weekend for three summers we twenty teenagers, Dorm, and our assistant scoutmaster worked all day, cooked our meals over open fires, and slept under the stars.

After three summers of labor (plus that of countless weekends during the school year) we had our log lodge in the woods.

It was an imposing twenty-five-by-forty-foot structure with a main floor larger than most of our homes and a massive fireplace built by the father of one of the boys who was a stonemason. It had a large kitchen and a sleeping loft.

It is difficult to convey the extent of the work it took to build Sundown Lodge—or our sense of achievement in getting it done—to anyone who has never built a building from the ground up.

In the narrowest sense, it would be true to say that we learned to use a variety of common hand tools, build a complex structure, and grow calluses and a few scars where none existed before.

In a broader sense, we were witness to an example of

The lodge we built was big enough for all twenty members of Troop 511 and their parents to gather in. The physical structure of Sundown Lodge is long gone but the lessons we learned building it have spanned the generations. *Photo, 1939.*

visionary and inclusive leadership and the amazing power of people working together toward a common goal.

All the showing up Dorm did in our lives gave shape to more than a log lodge in the woods. It gave shape to a place in our minds where we believed anything was possible.

Hard Work

People often ask me why—at the age of eighty-three—I still rise early every morning and drive to an office to work.

I usually respond with a predictable three-word answer: I like working.

I like the challenge of having to make decisions where there's always a risk of failing. I find that exhilarating. I think I'm much better off doing what I'm doing than I would be sitting on a beach somewhere.

I suppose there are many reasons why I'm working almost as hard today as I did when I was a much younger man practicing law.

One of them has to do with my father.

In my first summer job during high school, I worked as a "swamper" in my father's furniture store, lifting such things as mattresses and sofas and easy chairs on and off of delivery trucks and carrying them into people's homes.

I put in long hours doing physically taxing work. And my father was pleased with how I attacked the job.

In 1912 my grandfather, William Henry Gates, agreed to pay $733 to buy the stock of a furniture store on Front Street in downtown Bremerton. By the time I was born, the store, the U.S. Furniture Store, was being run by my father and my grandfather's partner's son, Roy Morrison.

As far back as I can remember my dad's life revolved around the store, but he never took things for granted.

My earliest memory of Dad is an image of him walking home from work every night picking up pieces of coal he'd find in the alley. They had fallen off trucks delivering coal to our neighbors. In those days people used coal to heat their houses. Dad would bring those stray pieces home and put them in our coal box.

This daily ritual spoke to the degree of anxiety Dad felt about making ends meet.

There was, of course, reason to be concerned. In 1929 when I was four years old, the stock market crashed and the Great Depression hit. So I grew up with a fear I don't think my own children ever experienced, the fear of ending up poor.

But my dad had learned something about what it meant to be poor long before the Depression. As an eight-year-old, he had sold newspapers in the freezing cold streets of Nome, Alaska, to help his family get by while his dad went panning for gold. As an eighth-grader he gave up school entirely to help support his family.

I suppose it was his history combined with the tough times we were living through that made Dad seem as if he was always running scared.

He didn't go to movies or ball games. He didn't fish or hunt or boat or hike. He rarely took a vacation until the day he retired. Dad worked.

In the early days of Microsoft, my son, Trey, and his partner, Paul Allen, worked, ate, and slept in their first office in Albuquerque, where they wrote software programs.

There were no days off in that situation either.

Trey worked at the same relentless pace for decades.

Achieving anything of real significance in life requires hard work.

My father sold his store in 1940 to a family from out of town that owned a much larger furniture operation.

The money my parents received from the sale of the store wouldn't have been much by today's standards, but it was more than enough to make them comfortable in those days. Still Dad's work ethic remained undiminished.

Even after he retired, he did stints working for another furniture store in town, along with helping on projects for his service clubs.

When my older daughter, Kristi, was a little girl, she sometimes took the ferry from Seattle to Bremerton to spend time with her grandparents.

She remembers walking with my mother to meet my father at the end of each day, down the same alley where he had picked up coal to heat our house in the depths of the Depression. Then as before, he was walking home from work.

Radical Generosity

My sister Merridy was seven years older than I. When we were growing up, I often felt uncomfortable about the fact that there seemed to be different rules for me than there were for Merridy.

One example of this was that our father didn't think girls needed to know how to drive. So, Merridy never learned how to drive a car. I, on the other hand, was permitted to get my driver's license the minute I turned sixteen.

By that time Merridy was married. She had a job and was earning her own money. For my sixteenth birthday, she spent eighty-five dollars—which was a significant sum then—to buy me a birthday present: a 1930 Model A Ford roadster with a rumble seat. Merridy's generosity—when she had been denied the opportunity to drive herself—was something I have never forgotten.

I was elated with the roadster. Dad was not. He must have spent three times what Merridy paid for the car to make it safe for me to drive, lending some credibility to the notion that "what goes around comes around."

Of course, Merridy's gift to me was more than a car—she gave me my first real lesson in what it means to be a truly generous person.

We've all known people a few steps ahead of us—whether it's a difficult older sibling or a controlling boss—who seem determined that no one else will ever make it to their station in life without undergoing the same pain and hardship they suffered.

By contrast, Merridy, who had never even been allowed to get a driver's license at my age, reached beyond the limits of her history, her restricted resources, and any inclination toward envy, to give me a gift she herself had never been given.

Open-Mindedness

Thinking matters through before we act is always difficult
and often consumes a lot of our time. But it is simply not
possible to be a person of integrity without doing it.
–Stephen Carter, *Integrity*

My first thoughts on the importance of open-mindedness came from observing the contrast between my mother's and father's ways of thinking—and the effect each sometimes had on others.

My mother was an open-minded person who didn't have a lot of fixed ideas about what my sister and I should do growing up.

Dad, who was somewhat insecure about his lack of formal education, found comfort in living by a number of inviolable axioms. Axioms on such things as the importance of hard work made perfect sense. But some of his other axioms allowed me to see, early on, the sometimes unintended harm caused by close-minded thinking.

One of his axioms was that "girls don't go to college," and that belief had a limiting influence on my sister's life.

Mark Twain made an interesting point when he said, "The surest sign of intelligence is an open mind."

All through my life, I have gravitated toward more open-minded people.

Of course there were other influences besides my parents.

One was a teacher and high school basketball coach named Ken Wills, who invited my friends and me to his home for weekly discussion sessions. He had strong opinions on sports and politics but most of all on religion. He didn't believe in God or religion.

While his ideas were somewhat shocking, his lectures planted the notion in our minds that we were free to entertain different people's points of view rather than just accepting the things we had been told.

Another influence was a psychology professor I had my freshman year of college, Professor William Wilson. Being in his class was a searing experience for me.

What made it searing was that many of our most fundamental assumptions, opinions, and beliefs were held up for analysis and critical scrutiny. We were asked to support our opinions with solid evidence and to question our assumptions by mounting logical arguments to the contrary.

Among the lessons I took away from that class were:

The fact that something is written in a newspaper, magazine, or book (or, in today's case, on a Web site) doesn't make it true; and there can be more than one valid viewpoint on any subject—and likely more than two.

I can tell you beyond a doubt that it was in Professor Wilson's class that I first became a thinking person.

There was a war going on at the time, World War II. At the end of my freshman year I would be ordered to report for active duty in the army. Learning to think for oneself was an important lesson for a young man heading off toward a war. And I can hardly think of any better lesson for a lifetime, really.

What I learned from Professor Wilson helped give me the freedom to think that I could challenge the status quo, focusing less on how the world was and more on how it ought to be.

Ever since then, I've tried to live my life that way.

In these last years, I've traveled to some of the world's poorest places and realized anew that a good many things are not as they ought to be.

In such places, it's easy to focus on how bad things are—so much so that you become overwhelmed by the challenge of trying to change them.

But I must say that what I see are mostly possibilities. Endless possibilities.

One of the nicest compliments I ever received was paid me a few years back by senior staff members of the Rockefeller Foundation and Rockefeller University.

I had been invited to speak at a conference on philanthropy that marked the celebration of Rockefeller University's one hundredth anniversary.

After the speech they told a friend of mine that it appeared I was "a gracious, intelligent man who *hadn't made his mind up about everything yet.*"

I hope they were right.

Of course, I was only seventy-four years old at the time.

Getting Along

In June of 1944 I received a letter ordering me to report for basic training in the army.

Not long ago somebody asked me what I learned from training to fight in a war. It's funny, but I think I learned a lot about getting along.

I learned I could "get along" in spite of physical challenge and discomfort. I could get along being in the heat and the cold. Get along crawling under barbed wire carrying an M1 rifle with machine-gun fire overhead and my ears ringing from the noise.

I also learned about getting along of a different sort.

My army buddies and I lived together in barracks with cots in a row on two sides of an aisle. We were a diverse group of people. With a war going on and a draft in place most healthy males between eighteen and forty-five were invited to attend—the rich, the poor, those who were educated and those who were not.

Though we started out as strangers, the difficulty of the physical trials we experienced together while pursuing a common goal built a feeling of camaraderie among us.

We all got along, and when it came to enjoying a beer together on a Friday night, where somebody came from didn't seem to matter much.

It was a nudge from the platoon mate with whom I got along best that helped me decide to go to Officer Candidate School. Having the encouragement to make that decision was probably fortuitous for me because by the time I was shipped overseas the war was over. Not everyone I knew was so lucky.

In 1945, shortly after Japan had surrendered, I was ordered to Hokkaido, the northernmost island of Japan, and later to Tokyo.

Tokyo had been devastated by the war.

On my walks through the city I remember being struck by the fact that despite all the devastation that had occurred, my encounters with the Japanese people there were so normal.

The kids would come up to us and try to talk us out of gum or candy or cigarettes. Nobody treated us as heroes, but on the other hand there was none of the hatred that might have been expected after years of war.

In Japan I learned, again, that sometimes in difficult circumstances people coming from significantly different places are, by the sheer force of their common humanity, able to view one another as fellow human beings and get along.

Speaking Out

The first job of a citizen is to keep your mouth open.
—Günter Grass

I first came to realize the importance of speaking out when I started back to college at the University of Washington after World War II.

At that time Senator Joe McCarthy was conducting witch hunts in search of Communist sympathizers and subversives on a national level. Other politicians were doing the same thing in my state and across the country.

Today, not many people get fired for their political beliefs. In those days, if you were suspected of being a Communist, you could lose your job, have your career ruined, and find yourself shunned by society.

Those of us who were older and had just returned from the service had fresh in our minds Nazi Germany's example of what the suspension of civil rights and political campaigns designed to silence dissenting voices could do to a society.

We knew a handful of college kids weren't going to stop what was going on in either Washington, but we felt we had to do something. So we started working to protect the right to free speech on our campus.

Students were concerned that there was a ban in force that kept politicians of any kind from being able to give speeches on campus. So my friends and I organized, collected signatures on a petition, and got that ban overturned.

Looking back, I think one of the most deeply rooted and enduring lessons I took away from those times was that each of us has an obligation to speak out about the things we believe in.

I've had many opportunities since then to observe people who are masters at speaking out in ways that generate real change in the world.

One of those is former president Jimmy Carter. President Carter, his wife, Rosalynn, and my wife and I were on a trip to Africa aimed at getting people there to talk openly about HIV/AIDS.

At that time, people's unwillingness to talk about HIV/AIDS and sex was getting in the way of communicating how the disease spreads and how it can be prevented and treated. It was costing people their lives.

I remember vividly one day when President Carter was speaking in a public forum in Nigeria and he decided to tell the audience something he'd just learned—that prostitutes in Nigeria charge more money for having sex with men who refuse to wear condoms, or, as he put it, ". . . with bare penises."

Given the nature and importance of the issues with which we are involved at the Bill & Melinda Gates Foundation, I am accustomed to talking about sex. Even so I confess to being startled to hear a former president of the United States use the expression "bare penises" in public. And that was precisely President Carter's intent. He wanted to shock his audience into acknowledging the important role condoms play in preventing the transmission of HIV/AIDS.

Later in the week we were in a church in the Nigerian president's compound where President Carter had been invited to give a sermon.

First, he told the biblical story of the woman who had committed adultery and was brought before Christ by a crowd determined to stone her to death. Christ's response, of course, was: "Let he who is without sin cast the first stone."

President Carter's message was that the Christians gathered around him should treat the victims of HIV/AIDS with compassion.

He then courageously soldiered on—in this Sunday

morning church service in a land where such things were never spoken of—to make the case for condoms.

What I've learned from many experiences—from collecting signatures for a petition in college to watching President Carter in action—is that there is enormous power in speaking out.

I don't care if you carry a banner or if you stand near the back, you can yell into a megaphone if you like, but each of us has an obligation to speak out on behalf of the things we believe in and make life on this planet a little better.

Learning How to Lose

If you compete for a prize and lose how do you react?

There was a time when I didn't react well. My best friend ran against me for student body president in high school.

He won. I didn't take it well. I was a sore loser.

Several days passed before I went looking for him, looked him in the eye, and congratulated him. My delay did not reflect well on me and I learned something I've never forgotten. There is no place in this world for poor losers.

Honoring a Confidence

Character is a tree. Reputation is its shadow.
—Abraham Lincoln

Some of life's most enduring lessons can also be among the most painful.

When I was in college a friend told me something in confidence that was very personal and important to him. He asked me not to say anything to anyone else about it. And I said I wouldn't.

But the story was so enticing that I couldn't resist the temptation to tell it to someone else. And before long, my friend's confidence wasn't completely a secret anymore.

The result was that I lost a friend. And I learned an important lesson: A commitment doesn't have to be written down in a contract or prefaced with an "I promise" to bear weight. Even social promises must be kept.

Many of us make commitments too casually.

If you don't intend to keep the secret or show up where and when you said you would, then don't say that you will.

It's important to be a person who can be trusted.

Finding Meaning in
Your Work

I consider myself fortunate because I have always found satisfaction and meaning in the practice of law.

A love of the law isn't about a statute book. It's about caring and being enthusiastic about having a just society.

I used to delight in going down to the courthouse in towns I visited to watch the young lawyers there perform in court.

I believe in the power of the law to help people and to change things for the better. And I believe most of us— no matter what we do for a living—have the power to show up and contribute something significant to whatever calling we choose.

While I don't remember the details of every case I handled, there are some things I'll never forget working with other lawyers through the Bar Association to achieve: Getting an inept judge out of office by campaigning for his opponent. Creating law school scholarships for students of color. Persuading citizens across the state to vote for a constitutional amendment to provide that the chief justice of the state supreme court be chosen on the basis of something more than seniority.

Working together, we also helped create an approach to delivering legal services to the poor that has endured.

These endeavors brought all of us who were involved with them some of the more meaningful moments of our lives.

Like many young people coming out of college today, I started out in law by going back to the small town where I had grown up.

My first job as an attorney in Bremerton wasn't rich in possibilities or glamour, but it was an opportunity to earn a salary practicing my profession.

Along with having his own private clients, the lawyer who employed me was also the city attorney. That gave me the de facto title of assistant city attorney, a title that sounds grander than the job really was.

I was involved in many of the kinds of work lawyers do. We did real estate deals, negotiated divorces, probated estates, and gave advice to businesspeople. And, once a week, at the local police court, I presented the city's side of cases that involved people being charged with everything from running stop signs to drunken driving.

My first job gave me a good start and useful preparation for the shifts and changes ahead. A career seems to unfold at its own pace and in its own direction without always being under the absolute control of its owner.

Some of the happiest people I know among my law school classmates took jobs right out of school and worked for the same firm their entire careers. A couple of others became professors at law schools. One fellow who was focused on civil rights had an illustrious career as a tax lawyer. And a woman who wanted to do estate work ended up with a divorce and family law practice.

What I learned from this is that life sends opportunities and challenges our way. And our futures are shaped by how we respond to them.

Sometimes the challenges and opportunities arrive together in unexpected forms, as with a difficult boss. I was surprised and embarrassed as a junior partner when a senior partner I worked with would lecture me on the shortcomings of his fellow partners.

Nevertheless, he was a master in the courtroom, widely recognized for his ability to analyze a situation, identify the heart of the matter, and build a compelling legal argument around that issue. I determined to learn everything I could from him.

In the end, I learned never to treat people the way he did. And I learned how to always set aside my own opinions and preconceptions to look at the matter from the opponent's point of view.

My daughter-in-law, Melinda, told me recently that when our family is vacationing together in the summer and we're sitting around the dinner table talking about an issue, they know in advance how I'm going to respond.

They count on me to reserve judgment and play the devil's advocate, asking them how they arrived at their opinions, how they know their facts are accurate, and if they've considered the matter from the opposite point of view.

There's been some suggestion that somewhere along the way my son adopted a very similar approach.

And so, all in all, I am grateful for the lessons I learned from a man I didn't always admire.

To celebrate my eightieth birthday Trey and Melinda funded a series of scholarships to the University of Washington. They are offered in my name to law school students who commit to going into public service law.

I visit with these young scholars several times a year. They are smart, caring people determined to make a difference in the world. I always come away from those visits inspired by the bold dreams they hope to fulfill as lawyers.

I know lawyers working all over the world who had similar dreams and who are now dedicating their lives to the ideal of equal justice. The powerful impact their work has on the lives of real people is evident in a story I like sharing with other lawyers about a woman named Amina Lawal.

Amina Lawal lived in northern Nigeria, and in 2002 she was at the center of a highly publicized trial in which she was sentenced to death by stoning because she had a baby out of wedlock.

Under sharia law, pregnancy outside marriage constitutes sufficient evidence for a woman to be convicted of adultery. No matter what the circumstances, the punishment can be death.

The man Amina Lawal claimed was the father of her child swore on the Koran that this was not true and he was allowed to go free.

The "crime" and the sentence aroused human rights activists around the world. The American Bar Association rallied lawyers here and abroad. Because of the public outcry that followed, governments pressured Nigeria's leaders to spare Amina Lawal's life. After almost two years of appeals, she was freed and permitted to return to her village to raise her daughter.

I remember reading an article about her written by a

I caught my first fish when I was seven and landed a memory that has lasted a lifetime. *Photo, summer, 1932.*

reporter at a time when her fate was not yet certain; he interviewed her as she sat holding and rocking her little girl. The reporter asked her if she had any dreams for her daughter's future.

She responded by saying that she believed her daughter's destiny was ultimately in the hands of God, but if she had her way, she would like her to be a lawyer.

Thinking Tall

Life is Niagara, or nothing.
–Mary Oliver, *Blue Pastures*

After the war, with so many men returning from the military and heading to college, if you were a fellow like me who loved to dance and you were looking for a partner, you faced a statistical handicap.

It was a little like that old Beach Boys song, *Surf City*, where there were supposed to be "three girls for every boy." Only after World War II, the odds were reversed. On the University of Washington campus at that time, there seemed to be about five guys for every girl.

So I decided to ask a woman I had become friendly with–Mary Maxwell–if she could arrange a date for me with one of her sorority sisters from the Kappa Kappa Gamma sorority house.

At six feet, seven inches tall, I felt more comfortable dancing with taller girls. So I made it clear to Mary that I wanted the girl she set me up with to be tall.

Mary was confident all along that what I really wanted to do was go out with her. She had decided I just didn't know that yet, or I was trying to ask her out in a backwards way. So one day we were standing on the sidewalk in front of her sorority house and I asked her for about the nth time, "Mary, have you got me a date from the Kappa House yet?"

She said, "Yes."

I asked, "Who?"

She said, "Me."

Startled and not knowing how to respond, I blurted out, "Oh, no, that won't do. You're too short!"

Coolheaded Mary, who was five feet, six inches tall, responded by turning sideways so I could see her profile, putting her hand on the top of her head, standing on her tiptoes confidently, and saying, "I'm not short. Look, I'm tall."

So we went out on a date and we married two years later.

Much later in her life when speaking to young people about their futures, Mary sometimes would describe the moral of that story: Never be afraid to think big.

"Never be afraid to think big" is a good description of the optimism and tall thinking that were among the keys to Mary's success in life.

When I first became acquainted with Mary Maxwell,

she was a smart, pretty college coed with an adventurous spirit. She was the only child of Willard Maxwell, vice president for a local bank and a respected civic activist, and his wife, Adelle.

Mary came from a long line of strong women. Her mother, Adelle Maxwell—later known to our children as Gami—was an extraordinary human being whom my son would one day call the most principled person he ever knew.

Mary's maternal grandmother, Lala, had long been widowed when I met her. She carried on positively and resolutely, living on a very limited income with some help from Mary's parents and by baking and selling cakes in the small town where she lived to make ends meet.

Gami and Lala were both role models for Mary and it showed.

In college Mary ran for student body secretary and won by a large margin. She was a fine athlete and a member of the college ski team. Mary loved competition.

Her buoyant, adventurous approach to life served her well in her first career, teaching. When she resigned because she was pregnant with our first child, Kristi, the principal wrote her a letter in which he described her as the best teacher he had ever encountered. After she left teaching she turned her talents toward building our family life.

Showing Up for
Your Family

When people ask me what I am most proud of in my life, my reply is always: "my children." And I say this convinced that the critical factor in their becoming the people they are today was the spirit of love and unqualified support Mary contributed to all our lives.

While our children were growing up Mary was always dreaming up ways of making our family life fun and interesting. Sometimes, to inject a little fun into doing the dishes, we played cards after dinner with the understanding that whoever won the card game didn't have to help with the dishes. We also made our own Christmas cards, together, and designed the invitations for the holiday skating party we hosted with two other families.

Mary was a master at creating events for us to enjoy with other families.

Our older daughter, Kristi, believes Mary created these

events because she thought it was easier for people who were not as extroverted as she was (myself and probably Trey included) to enjoy the company of others if there was a game to play, a skit to produce, or some other fun way to engage with them.

These events gave our children a large extended family to learn from and to love. They also nurtured a love of competition and let them cultivate the skills that I believe have helped them succeed.

In 1974—without Mary's knowing it—Kristi and our younger daughter, Libby, nominated Mary for "Mother of the Year" in a competition run by a local newspaper.

In her letter nominating Mary, Kristi listed all the things Mary was doing for the community. She also wrote, "There are three children in our family and even with all the time my mother spends doing volunteer work she has plenty of time left for each of us."

Libby, who was only nine at the time, wrote that her mother was almost always in a cheery mood, went to her soccer games, and took her bowling. In a postscript Libby revealed her own competitive spirit: "P.S. She'd better win!"

Mary did win.

She also won the admiration of many in the community she served.

Sharing Your Gifts
with Others

Mary started her career in public service by doing such things as tutoring children who were having problems in school and going into homes as a United Way volunteer to help a single parent and the kids get by after a mother or father had died or left home.

Over time the number of groups she served and the magnitude of her responsibilities grew.

She was a volunteer leader for Children's Hospital who lobbied officials in both Washingtons on issues affecting children, and for almost two decades she was a regent for the University of Washington. Her lifelong career with United Way carried her from being the first woman ever to chair our local United Way to leadership positions with United Way of America and United Way International.

On the United Way of America board she served

alongside such leaders as the president of IBM, John Opel.

In fact, it was Mary who first told John Opel that our son and his company, Microsoft, were working on a project for IBM. The venture between Microsoft and IBM occurred solely on its own merit. According to an IBM staff member, when Microsoft's work for IBM was brought before Opel during a review of the IBM PC project, he said, "Oh, that's Mary Gates's son." The IBM employee said it was nice that Trey's mom had put in a good word for him.

Connecting People

Mary was warm and genuinely interested in people from all walks of life. She always spent far more time asking about others' lives than she ever spent talking about her own. And because she was fully engaged with whomever she was talking to at the moment, the next time she saw that person she remembered the details of what she had been told.

I observed for years the effect that exchanges with Mary had on other people. She was so warm and interested in others that when people had a chance to connect with her, it could feel like the best thing that had happened to them all day.

Mary was quick to spot the special gifts of the people she met and was driven to connect those she believed could do more for society working together. There are organizations doing things like improving the lives of millions of people with cancer that exist, in part, because Mary helped to bring together the people who created them.

A former president of the University of Washington described Mary by saying she was "the glue that held the board of regents together." He went on to say, "Mary had a quiet dignity about her that affected other people."

Creating the Change
You'd Like to See Happen

When Mary became a member of the first cohort of women in America sought after for corporate board positions, her optimism and ability to focus on a bigger picture were especially important.

Rather than seeing herself as a token woman and acting accordingly, she viewed those corporate board appointments as opportunities to create the changes she wanted to see happen in the world. She worked hard, proved that she was diligent and smart, and earned the respect of her colleagues.

A Habit Passed Down

I believe our children developed the basis for their own approaches to public service, in part, by observing their mother. For example, Libby and Trey remember standing on a street corner with Mary on Election Day holding signs supporting a school levy campaign I was chairing.

Trey remembers working with Mary and me on political campaigns. And growing up around a dinner table where he was asked by his mother, "How much of your allowance will you be giving to the Salvation Army at Christmas?"

Celebrating Life

One facet of Mary's persona that shone through all her spheres of influence was her enthusiasm for life.

I remember one adventure we went on to the family farm of friends. It was a five-hour drive away from home and we arrived at our destination at two o'clock in the morning. Once we got the kids in bed, it was Mary who persuaded the rest of us to stay up all night with her to watch the sun come up.

Mary's well-known sense of fun was one reason our friend Meg Greenfield, a Seattle native and editor for the *Washington Post*, called us up one Fourth of July weekend. Meg had a vacation home on Bainbridge Island, which is a thirty-minute ferry ride away from Seattle. And she was entertaining Warren Buffett and *Washington Post* publisher Katharine Graham there that weekend. She wanted to bring her guests to our vacation place on Hood Canal to introduce Warren to Trey.

Mary immediately saw this as a great idea, and so she called Trey to ask him to come to Hood Canal that Friday to meet Warren. At first, he resisted, reminding his mother that Friday was a workday at Microsoft. However, being a dutiful son, he agreed to come.

That's how the extraordinary friendship that grew between Warren and Trey began.

Trey and Melinda arrived that day at Hood Canal, planning to stay only a few hours. They ended up spending the whole day.

In the spring of 1993, Mary started having an odd collection of symptoms including a dramatic loss of energy. Shortly after that she was diagnosed with a rare form of breast cancer. As always, she was optimistic.

Even so, sadly, by the time Bill and Melinda were married in January of 1994 in Hawaii, Mary was dying.

Mary's Wedding Toast

I remember helping Mary prepare a toast to Trey and Melinda that took the form of a letter to Melinda, based on the wedding vows. We cherish a picture of her delivering the toast, looking vibrant and beautiful.

Here is Mary's letter.

Dear Melinda:

In just a few hours you will be married and you and I will share the same name!

Although Bill and I have been married forty-two years, we continue to learn what it means to be married.

"To love and to cherish"

Celebrate his good points and remember you don't have to love everything about him. If you see some things about him that you simply have to improve upon (things his mother did not get just right) recognize . . . re-

My note of encouragement to the parents of any teenager is that with a lot of luck and hard work the result is a relationship with the love and admiration reflected in this picture of Mary and Trey taken at Trey and Melinda's wedding in 1994. *Photo by Lynette Huffman Johnson.*

forming a husband is a long term project and it doesn't always work out. Sometimes it is better to reform one's own expectations.

"For better or for worse"

Don't expect calm waters. Pray for courage. Keep your sense of humor. No man and woman ever had a perfectly harmonious marriage. A good marriage takes effort, resilience and suppression of personal ego, but the fundamental requirement is living with the fixed vision that your relationship is permanent and forever.

"For richer or for poorer"

 There have been but few couples for whom this phrase has had such special meaning. Every day will test the need for a sense of humility about your circumstances. Your lifetime together will, in the end, be a verdict on your recognition of the extraordinary obligations which accompany extraordinary resources.

"In sickness and in health"

 As you know in the last few months, we have had a chance to reflect quite directly on promises to stand by one another in sickness and in health. This challenge has brought a new depth to our relationship.

 Of course, the waters have not always been smooth, but I can't imagine not being married to Bill! I hope you will have this same feeling 42 years from now about your Bill Gates.

Love,
Mary

In delivering this toast orally Mary shared a quote from the Bible, the Gospel of Luke XII 48: "For unto whom much is given, of him shall be much required." This has become the basis of one of the two main values of the Bill & Melinda Gates Foundation.

Mary passed away on June 10, 1994.

Making Your Life
Your Message

As part of her mother's eulogy, our daughter Libby read a letter she had written to her two oldest children, who were so young at the time of Mary's passing that they would not be able to remember their grandmother when they grew up. It reads:

Dear Emmy and Steve:

You are a gift. It is because of you that I know how much a mother loves her children. I believe that a mother knows her child better than anyone on earth and no one will ever understand you the way I do. And secretly I'll never stop believing this. Neither did your Grammy.

She loved me, your Uncle Trey and Aunt Kristi completely and unconditionally— a concept I wouldn't understand without you . . .

I had asked her in her last few months of life to write for you, "Grammy's lessons on life." She was never able to do this project, so I am attempting it for her.

Lesson #1: Set every clock in the house 8 minutes fast:
This was your Grammy's complex method for being on time.

Lesson #2: The "dink" serve is the key to winning at tennis:
Her serve was so soft that it would barely float over the net. Many a time I watched her opponents wind up to smash a return winner only to hit it way out of bounds or into the net. Point Mary.

Lesson #3: Even when you're mad at your kids, if the phone rings answer cheerfully:
It drove us crazy when she did that.

Lesson #4: Treat everyone like they're important:
Your Grammy had a way of making everyone she met feel special. And her feelings for people were real.

Lesson #5: Take pride in your spouse.

Lesson #6: Remember that family comes first.

Lesson #7: Parent from a common voice.

Lesson #8: Give your children roots and wings:
    This is perhaps the most important lesson for me.
Your Grammy and Poppy did this so well. In our early
years they instilled in us their values. Then when the
time was right, they set us free.

Lesson #9: Have fun at whatever you do.

As Libby shared those lessons, it was never clearer that she is her mother's daughter. There have also been other occasions where I've seen our children express a mind-set reminiscent of Mary's.

In the early days of the Gates Foundation, Trey and Melinda began looking at ways to improve the health of children in the developing world, too many of whom were dying of preventable illnesses.

Shortly after they made their first gift to provide life-saving vaccines for these children, some doctors, scientists, and leaders in the field of immunology wanted to come out to the Northwest to thank them. Trey and Melinda invited them to their home for dinner.

Although these experts hadn't come asking for more financial support, after listening to them talk a while Trey asked them, "What could you do if you had more money?"

That really got them going on the topic of why some 30 million children weren't receiving vaccines.

Near the end of the evening, Trey thanked the experts for their insights and challenged them to come back to him and Melinda with breakthrough ideas for creating a better life for those children.

His parting words of encouragement to the experts that night were "Don't be afraid to think big."

Never Forget to Ask:
"Is it right?"

Find your conscience and hold it close.
–Allen Weinstein

No matter how humble or august our vocations, we're all human and none of us is perfect.

Many of us come to intersections in our work lives where there's a temptation to take a wrong turn.

Because I've spent much of my life practicing law, several real-life stories about lawyers who reached such crossroads come to mind.

One lawyer was both a co-trustee and the legal counsel for a $20 million trust left by one of his clients. The beneficiaries of the trust believed he had been overcharging them and sued him to get the fees reduced. As the case unfolded, a memo was brought to light that showed the lawyer had instructed associates at his firm to be aggressive about recording their billable hours for the trust. The beneficiaries won their case and the court removed the lawyer as a trustee.

Another was a young upstanding Seattle lawyer who, in the troubled time of the Watergate scandal, became one of President Nixon's White House plumbers. He was committed to the president and to a political cause. And so an ethical lawyer became a confessed criminal who went to jail for masterminding a burglary. He now spends his time lecturing lawyers and law students on the perils of crossing the line of ethical conduct. His message: "When you have a decision to make, never forget to ask: 'Is it right?'"

The final lawyer whose story I want to share is a law professor friend of mine who had a difficult choice to make early in her career.

When she was working at her first job for a large East Coast law firm, she was defending a business whose officers were charged with bribing labor union officials. The prosecutor alleged that this client would do favors for the union representatives, and, in turn, the union would send business the client's way.

My friend's job was to defend the company against a bribery charge.

While doing her research, she discovered among the papers in her client's file a cocktail napkin on which her client had written: "Buy [so-and-so] a new TV." The name scrawled on the napkin was that of the union representative.

My friend knew that although the napkin was evidence that could incriminate her client it had to be left in the file where she found it and, as the law required, passed on to opposing counsel.

The client was appalled by the idea. However, my friend and the senior partners of her firm insisted on doing the right thing.

The outcome of this story could have been different.

Since nobody else knew about that napkin, my friend could easily have "lost" it and no one would have been the wiser.

In each of our lives, we have opportunities to do many things when no one is watching. And it is under such circumstances that we express and cultivate character. We all make mistakes. But, as the classics attest there is nothing in life worth surrendering the right to think of oneself as a good person.

There are intersections of integrity and temptation in every career and every life. The challenge is to do the right thing no matter what.

The Power of One

I have witnessed countless instances where a group of people willing to work selflessly together in the service of humanity have effectively changed things for the better.

I have also seen instances where it took only one person to make a huge difference for mankind.

Such is the case with a fellow lawyer, teacher, and good friend of mine named Roy Prosterman.

His story provides an eloquent answer to a question most decent people ask themselves at one point or another in their lives, which is "What can *I* do?"

Roy knew that the vast majority of the world's extreme poor—those who live on less than a dollar a day—are farmers who don't own the land they work. And he recognized a simple truth: When families own the land they farm, they work harder, invest more in it, and make their land more productive. In doing so, they can lift themselves out of poverty and go on to make economic contributions to their community.

So he founded a group called the Rural Development Institute to pursue that deceptively simple formula for land ownership rights.

The result is that RDI has made a difference for families, for communities, and for nations.

In its first forty years the work of the Rural Development Institute in more than forty countries has helped secure land rights for more than 400 million of the world's poorest people. In those same years, RDI established offices in China, India, and Indonesia while also working in Africa, Russia, and other countries of the former Soviet Union.

RDI's work involves many partners, including host governments, international donors, foundations such as ours, aid agencies, and local non-governmental organizations. The heroes Roy acknowledges are the leaders of nations who embraced solutions to protect and strengthen land rights for their poorest citizens.

RDI itself remained a lean, low-overhead organization. During those first forty years, its staff numbered no more than twenty-three, including nine attorneys.

The first large-scale demonstration of the power

of Roy Prosterman's ideas occurred when the U.S. government asked him to apply his land reform concepts in Vietnam. During the Vietnam War, their goal was to stem Viet Cong recruitment among the rural poor.

The result of Roy's investigations was legislation establishing what was called the Land to the Tiller Program, designed to extend land rights to one million tenant farmers so they could feed their families. The program was successful. Viet Cong recruitment was reduced by 80 percent and rice production increased by 30 percent.

Afterwards, Roy began to get requests for ideas and help from other countries around the world. For years he had conducted his work from two small rooms in the University of Washington Law School, with the help of a part-time secretary and a student research associate. Now RDI has matured into a formal organization with an independent board of directors.

Roy Prosterman provided proof that land ownership and ownership rights are a powerful force in helping to eliminate poverty, extend ownership rights to women, improve crop yields, provide better care for the land, and stimulate economies.

The growing impact and acceptance of RDI is evidenced by the fact that the programs they help design are receiving substantial funding from governments that want to support land reform activities.

Beyond all that, he demonstrated to all of us, and to millions more around the world, that a single individual with boundless passion for a good idea can change lives for the better.

Things I Learned from My Children

It goes without saying that children learn the most by watching their parents in action. But the reverse is also true. If we pay attention, parents can learn a great many things from observing our kids. Here are some things I learned from my children.

I learned about competence from my daughter, Kristi.

The oldest of my three children, she is thought to take after me. We both prefer quieter pursuits and enjoy most the company of a handful of intimate friends. We relate better to our children when they become old enough to hold their own in a conversation. We're also thought to be harder on ourselves than is necessary. In my eyes Kristi's defining characteristic is her extraordinary competence—which continues to show itself in every area of her life.

Our first clue that Kristi was going to be a person who set high standards appeared when she was five years old. She would sit in the backseat of the car and complain that I was driving too fast.

Kristi was meticulous, conscientious, and self-disciplined to a degree that is rare for a child. She also had a built-in compulsion for following the rules.

While Kristi had high expectations for all of us—typical of an oldest child—she held no one to higher account than herself.

For example, shortly after she had acquired her driver's license, Kristi was preparing to drive somewhere. She went out into the garage, got in the car, and backed the car out of the garage, not realizing Mary's mother's car was parked in the driveway. She backed the family car into her grandmother's car.

She was so distraught about what she felt was her complete incompetence that she drove the car right back into the garage. Then she went back in the house and down the stairs to her bedroom and cut up her driver's license!

I'm happy to report that today she is a terrific driver and one of the most competent persons I know.

Given her strengths, she chose the right vocation—one that Mary and I first had inklings of when she was about ten.

At that time, we all went on a family road trip to Disneyland. Kristi wanted to take her own spending money. This consisted of ten dollars from her savings account and ten dollars her grandmother had given her.

Along with the money, she took a little notebook with her to keep track of how she spent her money.

Shortly before we arrived back home, she opened up the book to see how much money she should have left according to her notes. Then, she opened up her purse and counted her money. The two sums matched to the penny. It was then we realized that Kristi might grow up to be an accountant.

And that's exactly what she did. After she graduated from college, she went to work as a certified public accountant with Deloitte, one of the Big Eight accounting firms then and one of the Big Four today, and ultimately became a partner.

Kristi always was determined to make her own way in life.

As a college girl she began to realize that everywhere she went in her hometown she was "Mary Gates's daughter." She didn't want to be known as either her mother's daughter or Bill Gates's sister. To make a fresh start on their married life, she and her husband, John Blake, made their home in Spokane, Washington.

Quite independently, she became a force in her com-

Kristi and her husband John Blake built their lives in Spokane, Washington, five hours and a world away from Seattle where she grew up. They are shown here on their wedding day in 1987.

munity and president of their United Way while working as the accountant who did her brother's taxes, raising two children—Kerry and Sully—and living a full life with her husband.

Thanks to her competence and credentials in business and finance, she has become a director of a public utility and three companies. She is on the University of Washington board of regents, where I also serve. I'm sure any parent can relate to the pride I feel seeing Kristi's competence in action, doing this important work.

It is also moving for me to hear her say that she is in-

My daughter Kristi's continuing drive for perfection did not keep her from enjoying a near perfect day. *Photo, 1957.*

spired every day by the memory of the self-discipline and diligence she saw her mother put forth as Mary spent long, intense hours doing similar work.

Kristi's competence as an older sister is evident in the fact that she is fiercely loyal to her siblings and good at holding confidences, as I recently discovered.

When Kristi's brother, Trey, was in junior high school he regularly would sneak out of the house at night and onto the University of Washington campus to work on computers with his friend Paul Allen. They had landed a job with a company located not too far from our house that was paying them to test the security for their mainframe computers by trying to hack into the system.

Mary and I had no idea our son was out late on school nights living a second life as a hacker. Kristi knew but never betrayed her brother's trust.

As she said to me recently, "That basement was *easy* to sneak out of. I just never did it."

I guess I could ask Libby if *she* ever snuck out at night, but why ask if you think you might not like the answer?

Like every other parent, at times I worried about my own competence as a dad. So much was going on—apparently including some things I didn't know about.

I am intrigued by the fact that most of us seldom look for any guidance on how to perform competently as parents when there is so much good formal training and information available.

Mary and I took one Parent Effectiveness Training course together at our church. It wasn't nearly enough. Even so, I still remember a lesson from that class worth passing on. "No matter what you do, never ever demean your child."

I have often said that the most rewarding part of my life—by far—has been raising children and being part of a family. I suspect that's true for many of us, especially if we define *family* broadly so that the term includes blood relatives, adopted family, and even those with whom we have special bonds of affection.

So my advice to those who are considering becoming parents is to make every effort to make your performance in that role count.

Show up as a parent by learning everything you can about parenting. Show up by thinking carefully about the kind of parent you want to be and what it will take to achieve that goal.

Becoming a truly competent parent might be the most important work you ever do.

I learned from Trey that childhood curiosity can last a lifetime.

When Trey was very young I often took him to the library. He loved to read and often needed to return the books he'd read to check out more.

I know many parents would love to entice their children into becoming readers. So let me report that it's possible to take even the best of good habits a little too far. One unintended consequence of all those trips to the library was that Trey read so much he was reading at the dinner table!

Mary and I did our best to convince him that, in light

of certain social proprieties, reading while dining with others was not a good thing.

One contributor to Trey's nonstop reading was the fact that every summer the teachers at his school gave their students a summer reading list and there was a contest to see who could read the most books. Trey was so competitive he always wanted to win and often did.

Still, I believe the main reason Trey read so obsessively was that he was so curious. He didn't just want to learn about some things. He wanted to learn about everything.

We tried to nurture our children's curiosity in ways I think many parents do.

We didn't allow the children to watch much television, but we let them buy plenty of books. And it's true that we didn't enforce bedtime as strictly if one happened to be reading late.

If an unfamiliar word came up at the dinner table, one member of the family always walked to the nearby den, opened up the mammoth dictionary there, looked up the word, and read the definition out loud. In Trey's mind, this reinforced the notion that if you have a question, the answer exists somewhere. All you have to do is go find it.

Trey performed well in school. In fact, his teachers exulted in him. And I don't think Mary and I realized how much he was learning from his experiences. A case in

For Trey, Cub Scouts was more than gathering around campfires and eating toasted marshmallows. Every year, the boys went door-to-door selling nuts to raise the money for their activities. This was Trey's first experience with the world of commerce. *Photo, 1966.*

point is the experience that marked his first brush with the world of commerce—selling nuts.

That's right. When Trey was a Cub Scout, his troop earned the money they needed to support their activities by selling raw nuts for the holidays. Groups within the pack competed against each other to see who could raise the most money. So Trey spent countless hours going door to door soliciting orders for nuts.

On evenings and weekends, I went with him, driving him to different neighborhoods and waiting in the car while he went from house to house.

It turns out that way back then Trey was recording his impressions on such things as what it's like to go knocking on doors trying to sell a product, what factors influence buying decisions, and to what degree finding the right market for your product influences your overall success.

By the time he was entering his teens Trey's curiosity had led him to another activity from which he was learning a great deal—spending time in his school's computer room with his friend Paul Allen.

While still in school Trey, Paul, and another friend developed their first entrepreneurial venture: a company that created and marketed a piece of equipment they had developed called the Traf-O-Data.

It was designed to collect and make sense of the information generated by those little car-counting devices you've probably seen hundreds of times—a thin hose stretched across a road and connected to a black box.

The Traf-O-Data took the raw data from all those little black boxes and created a graph that gave you an hour-by-hour picture of each day's traffic flow. It was a useful tool for anybody trying to make decisions about traffic routing and road construction.

After many successful kitchen-table practice sessions my son convinced some employees of the City of Seattle to come to the house for a demonstration.

Well, things that day at the Gates home didn't go according to plan.

The Traf-O-Data did not perform.

How did Trey react when his first live demonstration of his system failed?

He went running into the kitchen, shouting on the way: "Mom, Mom . . . come and tell them that it worked!"

It's probably no surprise that he made no sale that day! The Traf-O-Data did finally achieve some success, although it didn't foreshadow anything like a Microsoft.

Perhaps another lesson here is that every success involves a few false starts.

It seems that there was at least one other very curious person in Seattle. Years before they founded Microsoft, Trey and Paul Allen were studying how highly successful people achieved success.

Trey gathered intelligence on that topic at home around the dinner table. When he was growing up, Mary and I had friends, many of whom we'd known since college, who were achieving distinction in a variety of fields—from science and medicine to public service and business. When we invited these friends to dinner, they spoke passionately about their endeavors, and the kids picked up a great deal just by listening to them and, in Trey's case, by asking them questions.

Of course, Trey's questions weren't reserved for guests only.

When Mary was working on the United Way committee that decides how the organization allocates money to nonprofits, Trey would barrage her with questions: "Mom, what needs aren't being met? What other problems contribute to this problem? Who's trying to meet them? What results are they getting? How do you measure that?"

Trey's curiosity and his loyalty to deep analytical thinking have never wavered.

When he and Paul started Microsoft he instituted a tradition he called "Think Week." This was time Trey spent mostly alone doing his most serious creative thinking about the company.

I say "mostly alone" because when Mary's mother was alive, he spent Think Week with his grandmother, Gami, at her home on Hood Canal. She would cook for him and be there when he wanted company.

Trey remains as much of a reader today as when he

One of the great things about Trey and Melinda is that they can make each other laugh. In this case, it's on their wedding day while Trey cuts the cake. *Photo by Lynette Huffman Johnson.*

was a child. He doesn't read anymore at the dinner table—and that's a good thing because some of the books he's attracted to are increasingly unappetizing. They have titles such as *The Eradication of Infectious Diseases, Mosquitoes, Malaria & Man,* or *Rats, Lice, and History.*

He seems to remember everything he reads and is, at times, eager to share what he's learned with the next person he encounters.

His wife, Melinda, says one downside of this is that sometimes when he approaches people at a cocktail party they bolt because they're afraid he's going to start talking about tuberculosis!

Bill and Melinda met after Melinda joined Microsoft, fresh out of Duke University with a master's degree in business administration. They have three children—Jennifer, Rory, and Phoebe.

Trey collected his own college degree long after he and Melinda were married. He had dropped out of college in 1975 as a Harvard sophomore. The impetus had come from a phone call he made from his dormitory room to a company in Albuquerque, New Mexico, that had begun making the world's first personal computer.

Paul Allen, who was living nearby in Boston at the time working for Honeywell, had seen an article on the new computer in *Popular Electronics* magazine and rushed over to show it to Trey. They had been expecting that personal computing would arrive and that when it did software would be a critical ingredient.

So when Trey called the company making the computer he offered to sell them software. The company immediately expressed interest, opening the door to Trey and Paul's marvelous adventure with Microsoft.

Of course Mary and I were sick when Trey told us he planned to leave college to take advantage of a window of opportunity he believed would be long gone by the time he graduated from Harvard. However, he promised us that he would go back to Harvard, "later," to get his degree.

"Later" finally arrived thirty-two years down the road on June 7, 2007, the day Harvard awarded Trey an honorary Doctor of Laws degree. I traveled to Cambridge with him and Melinda to watch him collect his honors and deliver Harvard's commencement address.

After the appropriate acknowledgments, Trey told the audience, "I've been waiting more than thirty years to say this." Then he looked out into the audience, directly at me, and said, "Dad, I always told you I'd come back and get my degree."

Perhaps there's a lesson in this for the parents of other curious children who, from the start, require the freedom to meet life on their own terms. It is that there is no statute of limitations on the dreams you have for your children. And there is no way to predict how much delight you might feel when those dreams are realized in a far different way than you could have imagined.

On the occasion of Trey's fiftieth birthday, I wrote him a letter. In it, I told him I believed his curiosity has had much to do with his success.

I told him that the rewards associated with having him for a son were too numerous to fit on a single page. I concluded with a more succinct description of the feelings I have about being his father. It follows.

Over time, I have cautioned you and others about the overuse of the adjective "incredible" to apply to facts that were short of meeting its high standard. This is a word with huge meaning to be used only in extraordinary settings. What I want to say, here, is simply that the experience of being your father has been . . . <u>incredible</u>.*

I learned about the force of confidence and heart from my daughter, Libby.

Someone once said that the purpose of life is to surprise us. The birth of our younger daughter, Libby, was one of life's surprises.

Once we learned Mary was pregnant, the entire family was excited. Kristi and Trey were totally focused on the coming of a new baby.

Because Kristi was ten and Trey was almost nine when Libby was born, they related to her with the guiding hands more typical of an aunt and uncle—or an extra set of parents—than of a sister and brother.

Mary and I always believed their contributions to Libby's self-worth and sense of comfort with the world

---

*Incredible—too extraordinary and improbable to be believed.

helped her cultivate one of her most distinguishing characterics as a child: her extraordinary self-confidence.

Her extra measure of confidence was in full evidence when she played soccer. Libby was a goalie.

Mary and I spent many hours standing on soccer fields watching Libby's games, and one thing we noticed was that many young goalies cried when they were criticized by their teammates if the other team scored. Libby didn't do that. Even when she missed the ball, she took the pressure in stride. She knew she was a good goalie.

Like her mother, Libby was a gifted athlete who was lovely to watch. She earned twelve letters in high school, won the state championship in tennis doubles, and captained the softball, basketball, and tennis teams.

By the time she was a sophomore at Pomona College in California, she was a starter on the varsity basketball team and remained one throughout college.

Libby's relationship with her grandmother also may have contributed to her sense of herself. Libby spent every summer through high school at her grandmother's place on Hood Canal. There, she cultivated her own friends and—when she was old enough—held summer jobs washing dishes at a café and being a bus girl at a local resort. Mary and I visited on weekends, but Libby enjoyed a lot of independence.

Libby and her husband Doug Armintrout have the kind of family I think most anyone would like having in their neighborhood. I feel fortunate that they live in mine. *Photo, Hood Canal, 1990.*

After finishing college and participating in the effort to create Seattle's Goodwill Games in 1990, Libby married Doug Armintrout and started her own family. Doug and Libby have since been raising their own three children—Emmy, Steve, and Mary—just up the street from me.

Her current athletic pursuits still speak to her high level of confidence.

She coaches her son at basketball, having earned the acceptance of the other boys' dads. She plays tennis with

The best games mimic life, with ups and downs, wins and losses, and quick thinking combined with equally quick physical response. Libby is a natural athlete, and has always enjoyed the mental and physical challenges of any sport—whether it was softball, soccer, or basketball. *Playing softball, 1985.*

her brother, Trey, who is intensely competitive and plays a formidable strategic game.

Although she is by her own assessment not a good swimmer, she also competes in triathlons where she rides a "very mediocre" (low-cost) bicycle without the performance-enhancing advantages of the latest technology.

Libby's penny-wise approach to purchasing athletic equipment didn't begin with her bike. It is legend in our family.

Shortly after Microsoft became a household word, Libby went to buy a new pair of skis. When she gave the clerk at the sporting goods store her credit card he saw the name on the card and asked if she was any relation to Bill Gates.

She said, "No."

He said, "I didn't think so, because if you were, you would have bought a better pair of skis!"

The fact is she didn't think she needed more expensive skis.

Her leadership style—first shown on athletic fields—has begun to distinguish Libby in other arenas.

She has led the board of trustees for her alma mater, Lakeside School, and is a trustee at Pomona College. She is also a volunteer leader for many of the same organizations her mother served. And her confidence continues to show.

I have heard from those who work with her that, as a leader, she is unflappable in the face of controversy. She listens to competing voices then works to unite those who disagree and help vest them in the ultimate decision.

She's able to do this in part, I think, because Libby isn't dependent on compliments. She trusts her instincts in a way that is reminiscent of a little girl I once watched on a soccer field.

Those outside the family say that Libby reminds them a lot of Mary. This is not a surprise to us because we have always known that, along with her mother's athletic talent, Libby inherited her mother's heart.

From the time she was a little girl it was clear that Libby had Mary's easy way with people and a similar way of radiating warmth and the genuine delight she feels in the presence of others. Libby has also consistently demonstrated a willingness to follow her heart. One of the first causes of her heart was the Make-A-Wish Foundation, which is dedicated to fulfilling wishes for children who are dying. She befriended a wonderful little girl named Lissy Moore who was suffering from cystic fibrosis.

Lissy's wish was to meet Michael Jordan. This was not an easy wish to fulfill. But Libby pursued Michael Jordan for Lissy, later admitting that her trademark composure was entirely blown the day she answered her cell phone and heard "Hello Libby, this is Michael Jordan."

The reward, of course, was that after two years of waiting, Lissy met Michael Jordan, who wrote a letter to Make-A-Wish saying what an inspiration Lissy had been to him and how glad he was she'd touched his life.

When Lissy passed away at the age of fifteen, Libby was asked to speak at her funeral.

One lesson I've learned from watching Libby is that if we can summon the confidence to follow our hearts and rise to the occasion even when it involves going where it hurts, we can make a lot of wishes—our own and those of others—come true.

The Enduring Campfires
of Cheerio

When our two oldest children were young, Mary and I happened onto an idea for a family tradition my children say greatly influenced their outlook on life.

In the summer of 1957, a law partner of mine asked Mary and me to visit his family at Hood Canal—on Washington's Olympic Peninsula—to have a campfire dinner with them and a group of six other families.

These families, whose children were now teenagers, had vacationed together for many summers at Hood Canal at a small resort called "Cheerio."

Listening to them recount their shared adventures at dinner, Mary came up with the idea that we should adopt their tradition and start our own summer idyll at Cheerio.

We launched it the following summer—when Kristi

was four and Trey was three—by inviting six other families to join us.

Everybody enjoyed the experience so much that we decided to do it again the following summer, and then the next one, and the next, until fourteen summers had passed. Along the way, we added a few more families, so there were eventually eleven families in all spending two weeks together every summer.

Cheerio was situated on a large, partially forested site that had a generous stretch of beachfront on the canal.

Both the grounds and lodgings at Cheerio were decidedly rustic.

There were eight wood cabins, later ten, plus one traditional log cabin with a large fireplace that made it one of our favorite places to gather. And there was a dilapidated tennis court that had grass growing up between cracks in the concrete.

What Cheerio lacked in luxury it made up for in price point, and it had all the outdoor space we needed to stage a unique combination of group events.

Every family had certain things they were really good at. The events we held at Cheerio gave each one a chance to demonstrate its talents and to discover the capabilities of the others.

One dad was a good tennis player. So every summer

he staged a tennis tournament that gave both kids and adults a chance to compete at tennis and improve their skills.

A number of other parents created Cheerio's Olympic Games, featuring such events as a three-legged race and an egg-on-the-spoon run. The games culminated with an Olympic-style awards ceremony. We acquired some inexpensive ribbons and built a stage that was a replica of the real Olympic awards platform. When the victors climbed atop the platform to claim their awards, the crowd cheered.

Some of the sports the children engaged in—tennis, swimming, and waterskiing—called for physical coordination. Other pastimes required only a willing spirit.

Those ranged from marching in parades behind a big gold banner with the word "Cheerio" emblazoned on it to participating in "Capture the Flag" or a game the mothers called "Round Rock."

Although the children never knew it, the object of Round Rock was to give the mothers time to relax together on the beach while the children searched high and low for the roundest rocks they could find.

A jubilant child might come running up to one of the mothers—rock in hand—and say, "Do you think this is a good one?"

A clever mother would respond by carefully examining the child's rock, administering a hearty dose of praise, and then saying, "But maybe you could find a better one." Off the child would go to look for another rock.

Hours passed this way with hardly a child realizing it. As one of the mothers remembers, "The children loved this game!"

The mothers of Cheerio not only shared the supervision of the children, each maintained high standards for child behavior. If a child misbehaved or uttered a bad word in any mother's presence, justice came swiftly.

The evening events at Cheerio were as entertaining as the daytime activities.

A couple of families shone at music; they brought such instruments as clarinets and trumpets to Cheerio and played them around the campfire where we performed skits and sang songs.

My children still remember the lyrics of a song we wrote at Cheerio. We sang it to the tune of the theme song from the movie *The Bridge on the River Kwai*.

We parents needed a ritual to help us get the kids to bed at night. So we'd get them singing that song at the campfire and use it to march each family back to its cabin, where we would wave good-bye and say good night.

As mayor of Cheerio, it was my job to lead the parade.

This was one of many rituals we repeated over and over again at Cheerio.

Another ritual we loved was the "Exchange Dinner." It was intended to give the children the opportunity to dine with parents other than their own mother and father. It began with a drawing in which each child learned the name of the couple that would be hosting him or her for dinner. The system was organized so siblings never ended up at the same dinner table. My children remember it as a great way to learn how to converse with adults other than Mary and me.

Other Cheerio rituals included a Sunday pancake breakfast and a parents-only party that took place on a Saturday night when all children were to be in their cabins by eight o'clock.

Every year that we returned to Cheerio the kids got better and better at the tasks they were learning there—waterskiing on one ski instead of two or improving at tennis. They also grew closer to one another.

The same was true of the adults.

On weekdays, most dads drove their cars onto a ferry at Bremerton and commuted across Puget Sound to Seattle to go to work, returning each night to a rousing welcome home in which the mothers and children ran to greet us.

In the beginning we dads only spent long weekends at

Cheerio. As the years went by, our long weekends extended further and further into the week. We cherished our time together as much as the kids did.

I believe Cheerio is a textbook example of the powerful role tradition plays in the rearing of children.

One of the marvelous things about traditions like Cheerio is the feeling of stability they give children and the memories they create. We remember being at Cheerio—crowded around a TV in the log cabin—the moment astronaut Neil Armstrong took his first steps on the moon.

From our summers of communal living, the children of Cheerio also learned many lessons.

They were able to watch a number of healthy marriages at close range and observe that not all marriages—or families—were the same. They learned that different families have different ways of doing things.

They also learned that everybody is good at something. And that you should look for that one thing in others and find it in yourself.

They learned that if you aren't good at a particular thing, you do it anyway.

And, if you compete for a prize and lose today, there's always tomorrow.

After the kids became teenagers and scheduling a joint vacation became next to impossible, we stopped coming together in the summer at Cheerio. But it would be a mistake to say that Cheerio has ceased to exist.

Decades after our Cheerio tradition ended and the children were grown, they flew in with their families from many different places for a reunion. Observing them together, it was clear that the bonds of intimacy they had established as children had stood the test of time.

My children say that living in community with other families for two weeks every summer was one of the most significant experiences of their childhood.

Now that they have children of their own, I watch them vacationing together with their families on Hood Canal, re-creating Cheerio-like moments with their own children.

Despite the passing of the years, they tell me they still feel the warmth of the connections they forged on those endless summer days and unforgettable nights around the campfire at Cheerio.

The Rites and Riches of
Lasting Friendships

To me, one of the most important things in life is friendship.

I still have friends I made in grade school. In fact, my first close friend and I (he lived next door when I was growing up) still make it a point to see each other.

And once or twice a year I get together for lunch with five friends from high school to reminisce about those wonderful days.

I believe it's important to be deliberate about nurturing cherished friendships.

Mary was a marvel at regularly creating interesting things for us to do with our friends—whether it was a volleyball game in the park near our house or a scavenger hunt or a costume party.

Almost sixty years ago now, she started a bridge club.

The club has met ever since, continuing on even after Mary's death.

One world-class moment in the life of the bridge club occurred the night my friend Charlotte made a point we all understood, without saying a word.

She thought her bridge partner was always too critical of and outspoken about her playing. So one night when he started ragging on her she pulled out earmuffs and put them on.

We all fell apart, laughing. And everybody got the point.

Rarely, are such heroic measures required to get your point across to an old friend.

Over time you reach a level of understanding and trust with your closest friends. You know these people, their prejudices and idiosyncrasies. You accept them, and you are even charmed by them. You sense that they in turn accept, uncritically, who and what you are.

To share a hearty laugh with friends you don't need jokes. You just need punch lines.

A lot goes without saying. And this is part of the inexpressible comfort of having an old friend.

During Mary's fatal struggle with cancer, it was the care and affection of such old friends that carried me through. And after she was gone it was they who filled in the painful empty spaces of my life. They were consistent and deliberate about taking the initiative to spend time with me.

Among them were some of the same couples whose families spent summer vacations with Mary and me and the kids at Cheerio and joined in on our family skating parties. After all the children grew up, we couples continued to make time for one another in our lives. We shared some vacations. We even went traveling and saw a little slice of the world together.

Some of these same dear friends are also in the bridge club. After all these years we are still very conscientious about meeting regularly, even though lately we decided that we will no longer play bridge when we're together. The friendships always were more important than the cards.

I find that to keep friendships alive one has to take pains to remind the people you care about that you're thinking of them and they are important to you. To me that means I need to mail that note or make the telephone call.

I've concluded that such attentiveness and deliberateness are indeed a small price to pay in exchange for the rewards of deep and enduring friendships that last a lifetime.

Learning Begins at Birth

Babies and young children think, observe, and reason.
They consider evidence, draw conclusions, do experiments,
solve problems, and search for the truth.
—Gopnik, Meltzoff, and Kuhl, *The Scientist in the Crib*

One great memory I have of my children's maternal great-grandmother, Lala, is waking up on mornings she was visiting and finding her and Kristi and Trey all piled into one bed in their pajamas reading together.

Reading aloud to each other is a tradition in our family.

On one trip we took to Disneyland, Mary and her mother, Gami, drove the family from Seattle to California, and I flew down to meet them later. They told me the long drive had gone by quickly because they all took turns reading a book about the famous racehorse Man o' War. They read aloud to each other—and then they discussed what they'd read. When I arrived, they had to tell me all about it, too.

Even though families have been reading aloud together for generations, the subject of early learning research is relatively young. I had never even heard of it until just a few years ago. I became aware of it in 2004 when a significant portion of the money requested in an education initiative was for early learning. I had to ask what it was.

Now I'm convinced early learning just might be the key to fixing education in this country.

My inquiries have convinced me that what children know—or don't know—before they ever see the inside of a classroom has a major impact on problems that can show up later on, including high school dropout rates, poor scores on student achievement tests, and the distressing matter of high school graduates who can barely read and write and who do not have the job skills required to prosper in a global economy.

Here are some facts that make the point. Children who don't attend pre-kindergarten are 70 percent more likely to be arrested by the time they're eighteen; girls who don't have positive early learning experiences are much more likely to become pregnant in their teens; *more than half* the children in my home state (and perhaps a comparable number in yours) are prepared only for failure the day they enter kindergarten.

Research shows that infants start learning soon after they're born. They soon recognize faces and respond to stimuli, especially love and attention; they mimic expressions on the faces they see; they laugh.

Later, they learn to enjoy being held and read to long before they comprehend a single word. I'm sure that Lala didn't realize she was an early learning instructor when she read to the kids. I'm also certain she was aware that the children were building vocabularies at an astounding rate and absorbing the fundamentals of acceptable behavior in their culture.

There is an entrance exam for kindergartners these days. A child isn't expected to understand fractions or spelling—but the better prospects will know the names of colors shown to them; they'll be able to spell a few simple words and their own names; they'll know their telephone number; a few will be able to read books written for the very young.

Now imagine what it must be like for a child who isn't ready for that first day of kindergarten. On one side of him is a girl writing her ABCs. On the other, a boy who can tell time.

This boy doesn't get any of it. Right away, school is a place where he feels like a failure, where he feels left out. When he goes home and his mother asks him what he learned in school today, he answers: "I hate school."

We don't have to guess what is likely to happen next to this child because we already know. He loses confidence in himself, hates school because he finds it humiliating, and, grade by grade, he falls further behind and finds others like himself who are bitter about their school experiences.

Think of the lifelong ripple effect of wasting the talents of that child. Then multiply that times millions of kids.

It doesn't have to be that way.

I've come to understand that for each dollar we invest in early learning, taxpayers stand to save seven dollars of the billions we spend on remedial education, prisons, and other social programs that intervene too late.

The world is a lot different now than when I grew up. Back then, most families had one parent working, one staying home. We lived close to other family members and our neighbors kept an eye not only on their own kids, but also on every other kid on the block.

Those days are gone. More and more families have two working parents because they must, and many other parents make a choice to follow careers they were trained for.

Intelligent day care by trained professionals at pleasant, safe places can be a reasonable substitute for many early learning activities.

There's no substitute for parental love and attention, and for a positive parental example, of course. But excellent day care can fill in some of the gaps, just as relatives and neighbors did in the past.

I think one lesson for us grown-ups is that family structures may have changed, neighborhoods may have changed—the *world* may have changed—but the way young children learn has not changed since the days when Gami and Lala and Mary and I read aloud to my children.

So it seems to me our job, as individuals and as a society, is to expand and support early learning programs *whether we have children or not* because learning in general, and early learning in particular, has a profound influence on our lives, our culture, our future.

Marrying Well (Again)

One way to sum up a lifetime quickly is to think of what would be the right words to put on your tombstone.

I think mine should read "He Married Well."

After my first wife, Mary, died of cancer in 1994, I met my second wife, Mimi Gardner Gates.

Mimi is widely known in academic circles as a scholar specializing in Chinese art and culture.

She is known in the international cultural community as the director of the Seattle Art Museum. In little more than a decade she oversaw the expansion and remodeling of the main museum downtown, reinvigorated the Asian Art Museum atop the city's Capitol Hill, and was the force behind the creation of the award-winning Olympic Sculpture Park in a spectacular setting on the city's downtown waterfront.

Along with taking on visionary and risky projects,

Here's what I would feel comfortable having people say about me a hundred years from now: "He married well." *Bill Gates Sr. and Mimi Gardner Gates, 1999. Photo by Florence Schandl Photography.*

Mimi is a leader who serves as a director on the governing body of Yale University, where she received her graduate degree. In fact, a deep and continuing connection to the lives of our alma maters is something we have in common.

For a couple that meets later in life, there can be some unique aspects of pursuing a courtship under the informed eyes of your grown children and lifelong friends.

When we first started dating, Mimi and I approached our relationship quietly because we both valued our privacy. But it can be difficult to conceal strong emotions from alert observers.

So I made it known to my family and friends how much I cared for Mimi. As one of my closest friends put it, "We were all beginning a new chapter."

Many families go through similar experiences, and it's my feeling that openness, tolerance, and affection lead to acceptance and help you fashion new relationships and move on.

One of the characteristics that first attracted me to Mimi (and I am sure helped her succeed in her professional pursuits) was her old-fashioned grit and determination. She likes to engage in what she calls "constructive rebellion."

Here are a couple of cases in point: When told by her father that the most important thing for a girl to do was to find a husband and get married, Mimi launched off on a demanding career of her own. And when told that women did not fly-fish, Mimi became an accomplished fly-fisher person.

She actually encouraged me to share the joys of fishing. In fact, we made a deal: If she'd play my game—golf—with me, I'd go fishing with her. That didn't work out as well as I'd hoped. She soon became a better golfer than me and I have yet to experience the joy of fishing.

Coming together in a second marriage involves not

only learning how to tolerate one another's differences, but also understanding how to appreciate those differences so they enrich the new life you share.

I know there are certain undertakings people often say new couples should avoid in the interest of maintaining equanimity in a new relationship. At the top of the list is building or remodeling a house together.

This did not hold true for Mimi and me.

When I met her, Mimi had fallen in love with a place called Shaw Island, part of the San Juan Islands scattered in the waters that separate the United States and British Columbia, Canada. After we became a couple, designing and building a home there, together, became a great adventure for us.

In talking about the options associated with design, style, space utilization, materials, and colors, we discovered a great deal about each other, and delighted in those discoveries.

Another important part of our new life that sometimes involved bringing together disparate opinions was a shared interest in art.

Mimi is an intelligent, informed, and active connoisseur. She invited me to share her knowledge and enthusiasm, and, far beyond our own walls, our frequent visits to museums and galleries to enjoy art have become a part of my life.

Our tastes are not always the same, and that has led to some wonderful discussions about what we like, and what we don't. And maybe that's the whole point.

Each discussion becomes an opportunity to discover more about each other, and to understand and appreciate each other's point of view.

Talking about what you agree and disagree on—talking, period—is essential. The older I become, the more certain I am that candid, objective conversations can resolve disagreements, prevent heated words, build trust, and deepen relationships.

One of the most important things I've learned about having a successful second marriage, or any marriage at any age, is this: It's never too late to get better at living with those you love.

Grandparents

I learned most of what I know about the important role grandparents play in the lives of children by observing Mary's mother, Gami.

All of our lives were made much richer and fuller by the contributions she made to our family's existence.

When my children were growing up and Mary began spending more time volunteering, her mother started coming to our house every day to be there when the children returned home from school.

Even though Mary's father had died by then and Gami lived alone, she almost never stayed for dinner. She was a very insightful woman and she insisted we needed family time alone.

Gami was a powerful and nonjudgmental presence in our children's lives.

Libby remembers that she was a true confidant, someone with whom she could share anything, and who could be counted on to harbor a secret forever.

Kristi regarded Gami as her second mother.

The fact that Trey went to his grandmother's house to do some of his most important creative work for Microsoft speaks for itself.

I learned so much from Gami about showing up as a grandparent.

I try to show up for my own grandkids when they're young by doing such ordinary things as taking one of them to McDonald's or appearing at grandparents day at school.

Mimi often goes with me to grandparents days, and often buys engaging books chosen specifically to meet each grandchild's interests. Something I've learned from her is that you don't have to be a blood relative to be a good grandparent.

She likes to tell the story of the day she brought one of our grandchildren to the Seattle Art Museum for a mask-making workshop designed for kids.

The instructor asked the parents and grandparents to step to one side of the room, and the kids to the other. My granddaughter just stood still. When asked why, she said, "She isn't my mother or my grandmother. She's my *step*-grandmother."

The instructor thanked her and then asked all step-grandparents to join the parents and grandparents.

We take each of our grandchildren on a vacation as his or her tenth-birthday present. The idea behind it is for the children to know us, and for us to know them. We think it works.

Lately, we've been taking one of our young grand-daughters to Shaw Island with us. And we've loved watching her share in a magical friendship with the little girl next door.

However, what it all really comes down to is this: I think grandparents—and aunts and uncles, for that matter—can give kids a sense of worth. What these adults tell children is "You matter to me. What you do matters to me. I want to see you. I want to keep track of what you're doing."

A Lesson on Leadership

I was once asked to give a speech on the topic of leadership at a Sunday morning church service.

I went through many drafts of that speech that reflected my analysis of the good leaders I had known and some of the attributes that made them stand out—attributes such as integrity or a gift for diplomacy, a willingness to speak out even if what they had to say was unpopular.

In the end most of my thunder that Sunday morning came from a last-minute idea I had to make copies of Lincoln's second inaugural address and simply pass them around.

This speech is carved in stone at the Lincoln Memorial and I will never forget the experience of reading it when I was there.

It was written in the latter stages of the Civil War—the

slaves had been freed, the North was certain of victory, and Lincoln was focused on the future.

In his book *Lincoln's Greatest Speech*, author Ronald G. White, Jr., makes many insightful observations about this speech and reminds contemporary readers of the enormous cost of that war. Civil War deaths almost equal the number lost in all subsequent U.S. wars.

In this speech, Lincoln could have focused the country's attention on the status of the war—Union forces were winning. He could have condemned the South and struck out at his detractors. But he didn't do any of those things. He spoke of a war he said both North and South had tried to avoid.

He referred to a North and South that prayed to the same God and read the same Bible. He called slavery a moral evil but warned against judging the South for it so "that we not be judged."

He spoke of caring for the widow and the orphan. Of binding up the country's wounds and of proceeding forward with malice toward none and charity toward all.

A woman said something to me at a tax seminar in Washington State that I think is a lot like the message I take away from Lincoln's second inaugural address.

I had just given a presentation on taxes in which I had said that the goal of the committee I was chairing on tax structure was to make our state's tax system more equitable for rich and poor while generating the necessary resources to meet human needs.

We were in a break-out session afterwards and a woman raised her hand and said: "So Mr. Gates, it seems to me like what you're saying is that *we're all in this together?*"

I now quote her all the time. In fact, this line has become my favorite axiom.

The fundamental idea here is interdependence. We simply cannot succeed without the contribution of others.

I think that's what Lincoln was saying in his speech: *We're all in this together.*

America at Risk

*If an unfriendly foreign power had attempted to impose
on America the mediocre educational performance
that exists today, we might well have viewed it
as an act of war.*

–National Commission on Excellence in Education

Ever since I graduated from law school in 1950 I have been involved with the issue of public education.

I've worked on levy campaigns, been on university visiting committees and committees led by business groups, and have served for more than a decade on the board of regents of the University of Washington.

I am concerned about the quality of education in America.

A 1983 landmark report from the National Commission on Excellence in Education, appropriately titled *Nation at Risk*, underscores my concern.

There is a dramatic paragraph in that report quoted at the beginning of this section. The full quote goes on to say:

As it stands we have allowed this to happen to ourselves. We have even squandered the gains in student achievement made in the wake of the Sputnik challenge. Moreover, we have dismantled essential support systems which helped make those gains possible. We have, in effect, been committing an act of unthinking, unilateral educational disarmament.

In considering this, one fact I find interesting is that the quality of our higher education system is considered the best in the world.

I think I understand one important reason why this is so. Being a trustee of a university, I have observed that institutions such as mine compete with one another as vigorously as players in any industry you can name.

They compete head to head for the best students, for the best faculty, and for the best facilities.

Rankings of universities and the schools and departments within them—though they sometimes are belittled—are mostly taken seriously and there is constant effort to improve these rankings.

In this highly competitive atmosphere pay and advancement are directly related to the quality of the professor's academic work and teaching skills. And there is always stiff competition for research grants and other outside funding.

A question: If our universities are so good, and competition is so paramount to the way they operate, might it follow that competition improves quality? It seems to me it does.

So what about pre-university education? I've looked at that, too.

Any analysis of our K-12 system shows virtually no competition whatsoever. No competition among teachers, no competition among schools, and no competition among school districts.

I say "virtually no competition" because as information about graduation rates and performance on standardized tests has become an element in public education there is a basis for comparison that is having some impact.

Some clear facts about the world of K–12 education in America: Schools can be judged and graded based on the performance of their students; teachers can be evaluated for their ability to teach and to motivate their students; our most talented college graduates are not interested in becoming teachers; around 40 percent of disadvantaged young people who start high school drop out before graduating.

The challenge is that the reform required is so fundamental. The profession of teaching K–12 must be revitalized.

Consider again what works in higher education, where

everyone is motivated. Why not provide similar incentives for K–12 education?

Teachers and administrators could look forward to rewards for work well done, and, conversely, poor performance would result in job loss or demotion. Another element not to be overlooked as a motivating force is respect from colleagues for doing a quality job.

I am optimistic these needs will be recognized and accepted one day, but I do not underestimate the challenge. Higher rewards for effective teaching certainly imply more than mere tinkering with the present compensation practices.

Public will for reform can arise when a school system is so disastrously bad that radical reform becomes acceptable.

A prime example of this phenomenon is New York City. Here the mayor, Michael Bloomberg, concluded that major reform was required. He personally took charge of the schools and hired a hard-charging former trial attorney to be superintendent. This reorganization was accomplished by breaking up several large high schools with two thousand or more pupils each into smaller units and engaging charter school operators to organize and manage the new schools.

One outcome: These new schools, serving the same communities, increased the graduation rate from 35 percent to 77 percent.

Another powerful example is Washington, D.C. A new mayor there was elected with an overwhelming mandate as the first candidate in history to win every precinct. His platform was school reform. He established a department of education, and when he did the local board of education and the city council lost direct authority over the District's public schools.

Another factor in the district was that the new school chancellor, Michelle Rhee, was a change agent extraordinaire. She closed some of the most troubled schools, fired a raft of principals, and let go hundreds of teachers. And she began awarding bonuses to teachers in schools where students boosted their performance on District tests.

They are attacking the problem in a meaningful way, although no one is ready to declare victory yet.

So there it is—two of the necessary ingredients for realizing progress: empowered central authority and effective management of the teaching corps that educates our sons and daughters.

Many parents, teachers, administrators, and communities refuse to admit to the basic flaws in their school systems. My optimism is based on what seem to me the lessons from revitalization of major city school districts such as New York and Washington, D.C. Reform will occur as the people insist on it.

The solutions to the problems confronting education in America require fundamental changes and drastic action. Getting it right will not be easy or comfortable. And getting it done will take broad engagement and support—from me and from you.

Four-Letter Words

Some four-letter words can halt polite conversation instantly, but the one that I find most destructive seldom causes shock or embarrassment.

That word is "mine."

As we work and acquire assets of various kinds, there's a tendency to credit ourselves for our successes and achievements. If we're generous by nature, we also may include at least some good luck and timely help from friends.

But all of that overlooks the obvious. Those of us who live in a free and open society owe a very large debt to our country as well.

To make that point I sometimes use the example of my son's success. I'm among the first to give him credit for hard work, a keen intellect, perseverance, a passion for technology and innovation, and a powerful analytical approach to work and life—all the characteristics we capitalists believe deserve reward.

But what if he'd been born in the mountains between Pakistan and Afghanistan? Or in Darfur? There would have been no Microsoft, no Bill & Melinda Gates Foundation.

My son had the good fortune to be born in a society that values education, individual initiative, and freedom of thought and expression; one that offers its citizens a wide range of mechanisms for the benefit of the entrepreneur, from a working legal system to key financial services, including access to capital.

One reason our view of life can be pleasant and expansive today is that we stand on the shoulders of generations who invested in the common good and in our future as well as their present. There's no question that we've been given a lot. The question is about what we give back.

Which brings me to another, even more powerful four-letter word: Ours.

Getting off the Sidelines

It seems simple enough to identify what can be claimed as mine and what can be considered *ours*. But deciding for an entire society can require more time and thought and debate.

Here's an example drawn from my experience.

One day in 1999 I stepped into an elevator in a Seattle office building and ran into an old friend. When I asked him what he had been up to, he explained that he had been working for a long time as a paid consultant on a particular issue. He went on to say that it appeared his work was finally coming to fruition in an act of Congress that now seemed almost sure to be enacted: the repeal of the federal estate tax.

His comment gave me a sick feeling.

I wasn't aware that there had been such a powerful and well-established effort under way to repeal what I thought was a fair and important tax and had long considered a matter of simple justice

I believe that a system of taxation where the wealthy pay in proportion to the disproportionate societal benefits they receive is the fairest way to finance our government. The citizens of most Western democracies seem to agree.

In the years I've advocated for the estate tax I've been reminded over and over again how important it is to study all sides of an issue and to get as many facts as possible. I admired and decried the cleverness of the repealers in referring to the estate tax as a "death tax."

I thought the more accurate phrase was the "grateful heirs" tax. This is a tax on heirs that is imposed—like so many other taxes—when wealth is transferred.

Once you get beyond the slogans, it becomes clear that the estate tax has been doing a fine job for the republic for about a hundred years. I have found no compelling reason to abandon it.

An array of sound arguments favor keeping the tax. Chuck Collins and I outlined most of them in our book *Wealth and Our Commonwealth*. It quotes the nation's founding fathers and many other notable thinkers who have argued for, written about, and advocated in favor of such taxes over the years. President Theodore Roosevelt, for example, spoke passionately about the estate tax's relationship to the ideals of equity and justice before its adoption in 1916.

Some argue for the estate tax out of concern that without it the citizens least able to do so might have to pay *more* so that the government can do the things we assign to it: build armies, roads, and schools, and more.

At the turn of the present century, we were uncomfortably close to having an economic aristocracy in this country with a widening gap between the very rich and ordinary citizens. As Warren Buffett, one of the richest Americans and strongest advocates of the estate tax noted recently, the groups at the bottom and middle are losing ground today and they shouldn't be.

That's precisely what I see happening if we repeal the estate tax. The rich would get richer; middle- and low-income families would find it harder and harder to move ahead. And that would strike close to the heart of the American dream of applying one's talent and energy to build a better life.

Government of the People,
by the People,
for the People

Here are a couple of thoughts about our government that you might not hear in a partisan debate.

Those who claim that the wealth they have accumulated is theirs to pass on without returning anything back to the American system show a shocking lack of appreciation for all that the system and public monies did to help them create wealth.

The role the government plays in a largely overlooked partnership that exists between government and private enterprise is a huge cause of business success. There are the highways, airports, and air traffic systems we all need and use—infrastructure we can see.

My readings also suggest that about half of the increase in our gross national product over the last fifty years or so is a product of new technology stimulated by government investment in basic research. Each year federal and state governments invest many tens of millions of dollars in sponsoring the kinds of research no venture capitalist would dare to underwrite—and the results of that research are made available to us all.

New products and ways of getting things done that benefit humankind and create the basis for the accumulations of private fortunes often trace their origins back to discoveries made over a period of time at one university or another. Many of these advances were achieved because the government has made continuous investments in basic research over generations, releasing its ownership of products based on discoveries created from research for which it paid.

The human genome, integrated circuits, and the Internet are three examples among the thousands of critical discoveries.

Every industry in America—from manufacturing to pharmaceuticals, agriculture, and the life sciences—has benefited from investments government has made in basic research.

Of course, these benefits extend to the building contractor hired to expand a dot-com's workspace and to the Wall Street broker retained to invest a software designer's assets.

The government also plays a huge role in helping prepare an educated work force.

So I believe that the government has the right to recover from the heirs to the fortunes of its most successful citizens some portion of those fortunes so it can keep this important investment stream going.

And I frankly question any value that flows from insisting that the children of our wealthiest citizens receive 100 percent of those estates.

There's a tendency to blame government and politicians for everything that goes wrong, and to resent paying taxes. Yet there's little tendency to thank government for the things it does well.

One lesson made clear to me again while lobbying for the retention of the federal estate tax is that the best way to learn what's good about our American system is to participate in it. We have to get off the sidelines.

I was greatly encouraged by the character and quality of the people I met in Washington, D.C.—senators and representatives and their staffs. And I include in this those who did not agree with me.

I feel strongly about this issue. I also recognize that as with the case of two old friends who met by chance one day in an elevator and spoke casually about their work, decent, well-meaning people will often disagree on specific elements of public policy.

What matters is that we exercise the rights and responsibilities of citizenship by staying informed and adding our voices to key societal debates. That is how we maintain the ideals that are at the heart of our way of life—and nourish those powerful forces of regeneration that renew *our* society.

The Older You Grow
the Taller You Get

People have some funny ideas about aging.

When my grandchildren were young—since I was both six feet, seven inches and the oldest person they knew—some of them were under the impression that the older a person gets the taller he or she becomes.

They were afraid my days of fitting in the house were numbered.

Looking back, I'm not sure their idea was so strange. On a good day, I could easily forget how old I am.

What often brings me back to reality is the name that the people at our Foundation have given me to distinguish me from my son. When I walk down the halls I overhear them saying, "Have you seen Senior?" or "Was Senior in that meeting?"

I was retired once with no thought whatsoever of a second career. Then one night I volunteered to help Bill and Melinda respond to the requests they had been receiving for charitable donations. And now here I am.

One good thing about growing older is that it gives life the time it needs to present you with unexpected opportunities.

⁓

Living longer is an unexpected opportunity many Americans have today that people in plenty of other places don't.

I think the average life expectancy of a typical citizen of Mozambique is in the neighborhood of only forty-seven years. Living into your seventies and eighties is mostly for the well-off and healthy.

So having seniors to worry about is a high-class problem for a society to have.

Seniors actually represent an enormous resource. Nearly half a million Americans over the age of fifty-five are volunteers for the National Senior Service Corps, serving as foster grandparents and in other roles. Hundreds more are in the Peace Corps.

We all know seniors who are the most dependable members of their churches and service groups.

Others have kept working or started second careers.

One friend of mine is a retired nurse. She recruits surgeons to travel with her to the Himalayan country of

Bhutan twice every year to perform surgeries on children there.

In my opinion, what often holds seniors back from doing more is not biology, but what we think of them.

Sometimes we're quick to spot the limitations aging imposes and miss its compensations.

In studying the relationship between age and greatness, author Melanie Brown noted that the history books are full of people whose greatest work was done in their later years—among them Justice William O. Douglas, the sculptor Louise Nevelson, Marian Anderson, George Balanchine, Georgia O'Keeffe, Alfred Hitchcock, Rembrandt, Bach, Jacques Cousteau, and others.

Dr. Brown noted that the painter Claude Monet had cataracts that distorted his perception, but suggested that he used that distortion to paint his glorious water lilies. She said that the delicacy, lightness, beauty, and softness of his paintings came not from perfect eyesight, but from perfect insight. Insight into the more subtle characteristics of nature.

My intention here is not to dismiss the challenges associated with growing older, for they are formidable.

I know well the frustration of being approached at an event by someone I know and having his or her name escape me.

At such times I can relate to the answer the late Bruce

Bliven, a former editor of the *New Republic*, was reported to have given when someone asked him what it felt like to be an old man.

He said, "I don't feel like an old man. I feel like a young man with something the matter with him."

All the same, I keep doing my memory exercises (which I hope are helping) and I am committed to an idea that bears a striking resemblance to my grandkids' notion of people getting taller as they get older.

It is that we never have to stop growing.

An Expression of Gratitude

The first time I was invited to speak before Microsoft employees at their annual meeting, I was facing thousands of young twentysomethings who probably viewed me as old and somewhat irrelevant.

I began my speech with the following opening line:

"Without me, you wouldn't be here."

They responded with laughter and gave me their full attention. I might even have summoned forth some feelings of gratitude.

And that was exactly the point.

I was helping kick off their United Way campaign and I wanted to inspire them to be as generous as possible.

One challenge in motivating a person to give time or money to United Way is that it helps many groups—some of which are not well known—and it touches the lives of people the giver will likely never have the chance to meet.

That's why, as I did that day at Microsoft, I often share an experience I had when I was chairing a United Way campaign and introducing the campaign's volunteer leaders to some of the agencies United Way supports.

We took those volunteer leaders on a bus tour to bring them face to face with some of the people they would be raising money to help.

One of our stops was at an agency called Transitional Resources for Youth, or TRY, which helps people suffering from the most serious forms of mental illness recover and succeed in life. Among other things, they provide housing and support for people who have just come out of institutions while they look for jobs and try to get their lives back on track.

When we pulled up in our little bus and I saw the place I was disappointed.

I thought: "This is such a small and ordinary-looking house that it can't be providing help for more than a dozen people . . ." I worried that the place would appear insignificant and not be a motivator for the volunteers.

As we went into the living room we were introduced to a young woman. She was dressed very neatly and my first assumption was that she worked for the agency.

She did not. She was a resident.

She stood up nervously to speak and told us about the ugly life she had led as a young woman with mental health problems. She had spent some time in an institution and had been discharged as ready to take her place in the outside world.

Now, to the credit of Transitional Resources for Youth, she had a job and was rebuilding her life.

She was exulting in something she had lost years ago—*a belief in possibilities.*

Since her job did not give her much time off, when she heard we were coming she took time off without pay so she could be there when we arrived. She wanted to thank us and let us know that, without us, she wouldn't be in the whole new place in her life she described that day.

I left that small house that day confident that our United Way volunteer leaders were deeply affected, as I had been deeply affected.

That young woman's story helped kick-start a record-breaking United Way campaign undertaken by that room full of young Microsoft people who were inspired by her expression of gratitude.

Traditions–Making Memories

I believe family traditions help give children a sense of continuity and permanence in a world full of change and uncertainty.

Nobody knows what's going to happen tomorrow or next year, but traditions are mileposts and monuments that bring predictability and shape and form to our lives.

Mary and I shared the conviction that it was important to be deliberate in organizing a family's life. And so we embraced some of both our families' traditions and created more of our own.

One tradition that first began at Gami's house was the tradition of Sunday dinners. The menu didn't vary: it consisted of roast beef, corn, and roasted potatoes. (Once Microsoft was started Trey generally arrived late, and ended up eating cold, well-done roast beef.)

One reason customs like Sunday dinners matter is because parents have a responsibility to socialize their children. And it seems to me that somewhere in between sharing stories and discussing the issues of the day children learn what's acceptable and important in their family. This gives them solid moorings and a sense of who they are.

I also think repeating rituals such as Sunday dinners communicates to children that it's important to show up for the people they love.

Sharing holiday traditions with family and friends makes the same point.

One of our family traditions is that when we assemble on Christmas morning we all wear matching pajamas. This acknowledges the memory of Mary and Gami, who delighted in buying everybody matching pajamas for Christmas and hanging them on the tree. It's also great memory-making material for the grandkids.

Of course, it is so often the small moments that occur while families and friends are partaking of traditions that leave the most lasting imprint.

When I was growing up, going to Hood Canal in the summers was a tradition in my family. When I was seven years old, I caught my first fish, a salmon. My mother took a picture I still treasure of me holding up my fish. But I probably wouldn't have needed the picture to remind me of this moment. Along with the fish, I landed a memory that day that has lasted a lifetime.

My family continues making memories today at Hood Canal.

On the day of Gami's memorial service, we all piled into my Ford station wagon and went out to look at some property there that Gami had told us was for sale.

Trey bought it and created a place where we vacation together.

On occasion the Cheerio Olympic Games, which we played when my children were young, have been re-created for the grandkids, although Mimi and I are finding it harder to run the relays. Competition and games have been long-held traditions in our family. In addition to being a way to engage with others, games have given our children an opportunity to learn to take risks in a safe place where all was not lost if you didn't win.

The Cheerio Olympic Games made a celebrated return during the first fifteen years of Microsoft's life, when our family helped Trey produce events he called Microgames. Those who attended Microgames were invited to compete on teams in a range of games and were treated to some good entertainment. The guests included both Microsoft employees and friends, including such old friends as members of the original Cheerio cast.

Like the events Mary planned for our children when they were young, Microgames nourished a spirit of fun and camaraderie among those who participated.

One longtime family friend of ours recalls that shortly after he arrived at one year's Microgames, he and his wife were directed to a table where the rest of their team for the event was seated. Eager to avoid being on a team that came in last, he quickly studied every person at his table, trying to size up the capabilities of his team-mates. One person who made him nervous was a very casually attired man wearing a mesh baseball cap. "Who is this guy?" he wondered to himself. "Does he have what it takes?"

His fear evaporated when the man in the funny, well-worn baseball cap introduced himself as Warren Buffett.

Traditions are important markers for moments in the life of any family. But life is a moving stream. Friends move away. Kids grow up. New people and interests come into our lives. So while there are traditions that remain and are repeated through the generations, there are also those that come and go. And it's been our experience that when they go, they are replaced by new traditions that bring fresh energy and excitement to a family's life.

Getting Everybody Dancing

People have often asked me the difference between what my life was like when I was a partner in a law firm and what my life is like as one of the managers of a large foundation.

The difference I noticed first was that when I practiced law people used to seek me out to get advice. Now, people mostly want to give me advice—on how to spend my son and daughter-in-law's money.

I sometimes have lunch at a place called the Burgermaster. It's in my neighborhood. After we started the foundation, that habit ended up getting me into the British tabloids.

A London newspaper carried an article about how I gave away my son's millions from a vinyl booth in a burger bar. It included a picture of me in a baseball cap next to a picture of the restaurant. For months after that I received mail from people all over the world at the Burgermaster.

Some of the letters the Bill & Melinda Gates Foundation received early in its life contained requests for help that were far beyond the scope of our mission.

One television viewer, for example, who became anxious watching a show about volcanoes, wrote us an urgent letter asking if we could vent the magma chamber of the Yellowstone Volcano.

Another fellow wanted us to fund a ballroom dancing channel so people from all over the country could learn the same steps on TV. He thought that way people on the East Coast could dance with people on the West Coast. And we could solve a lot of society's problems if we just got everybody dancing!

I wonder now if that letter writer had anything to do with creating my favorite TV show—*Dancing with the Stars*.

The lesson for me in all that mail was that most of those requests were from people trying to do something good for their communities.

Their letters really weren't all that different from one Bill and Melinda sent to me one day after they read an article that said people in the developing world—children in particular—were dying from illnesses seldom deadly to citizens in this country, such as measles, malaria, and diarrhea. They sent me the article with a note that said, "Dad, maybe we could do something about this?"

Shortly after that, working with others to provide vaccines to those children became a cornerstone of the Bill & Melinda Gates Foundation's mission. We chose vaccines because when you look at the benefits they provide, vaccines probably represent the most efficient and cost-effective tool medicine has to offer. Administering them a few times during the first year of a child's life can save millions of lives. With regard to global health matters, we decided our focus would be on prevention.

Whether they're working on providing vaccines to children in faraway countries, or putting computers in libraries so that even someone who can't afford a computer can go look for a job on the Internet, what drives Bill and Melinda to help is no different from what drives you to donate money and time to your community.

That wonderful spirit of neighborliness we share isn't unusual. The only thing that may have changed is our definition of the word *neighborhood*.

In today's world, our neighbors are not just down the street or across town, they are across the world.

We're all in this dance together.

Empowering Women

One thing my friend Suzanne Cluett and I had in common from the start was that each of us spent years volunteering for Planned Parenthood.

We both believed that enormous good is achieved when women are empowered and given choices. Choices about such things as how many children to have and when.

We also believed that families are likely to be healthier and communities better off when the children born are wanted.

Suzanne was a neighbor who raised her children just up the street from where Mary and I raised ours. But our friendship really developed when I asked her to come to work with me.

At the time the William H. Gates Foundation (a precursor of the Bill & Melinda Gates Foundation) was still a fledgling operation housed in my basement. We were just starting to identify causes to support that we viewed as ways of diminishing the world's suffering. And family planning was one of those causes.

Suzanne accepted my offer, working part time at my house and the rest of the time out of a hastily prepared office in a spare bedroom of her home.

So when things got very busy at the foundation headquarters in my basement and someone came to my house to request information, I would often point that person in the direction of Suzanne's house and say quite unconsciously, "Ask the neighbor lady."

Suzanne cherished the reference, but it was one for which I took considerable chiding from others because she was overqualified for her position.

She had from a very early age dedicated herself to becoming an advocate for the world's poorest women and children.

In college, she had yearned for a connection with the people in other countries. So she became a foreign exchange student. After college she began her career as a Peace Corps volunteer in Nepal.

Eventually, back in the United States, she became an officer for a group that makes modern medical advances available for people in poor countries. Suzanne also became known internationally as an activist for family planning.

As a young mother raising her family she had marched in pro-choice rallies with her young sons—Nate and Johnny—beside her carrying a sign they'd made themselves that said, "My Mother matters."

Suzanne lived by her beliefs at work and at home.

When her sons each turned sixteen she came up with her own way of heralding their transition to responsible adulthood. She emptied all the candy dishes in the Cluett household of candy. Then, she refilled them with condoms! Suzanne believed all physically mature young men should know about condoms.

While Suzanne and her husband, whom she had met in the Peace Corps, were both working and saving to put their own sons through college, they always maintained their relationship with the families they had known in Nepal.

Every other year they ferried baby clothes back to Nepal for the newest members of those Nepalese families.

When one of those kids—a girl—reached her teens and her mother, following the customs of Nepal, wanted to arrange her daughter's marriage, Suzanne challenged the mother. She knew the girl didn't want to marry. So she promised the mother that if she held off on marriage plans for her daughter, Suzanne would pay for the girl's education as long as she stayed in school. That girl went on to graduate from college and later married a man she loved. All the while, Suzanne was working through more formal channels to improve the lives of girls like her all over the world.

Suzanne and Dr. Gordon Perkin, our first Director of Global Health and a founder of the organization for which Suzanne had worked on developing medical advances for poor countries, were my guides on my early visits to poor countries. On these trips I was able to see, firsthand, the realities of how some of our neighbors around the world live. Suzanne also started our relief services, through which we respond when there is a tsunami in Sri Lanka or an earthquake in India.

All in all, Suzanne helped us forge connections and build alliances that delivered enormous amounts of help and resources to the causes we all cared about.

In 2005, Suzanne died of breast cancer. I miss her terribly.

A year after her death her family took her ashes back to her beloved Nepal.

There nestled in the foothills of the mountains is a large, modern, well-equipped shelter built in honor of Suzanne and her life's work. It is a place where expectant mothers can come and stay to be near a hospital right before and after their babies are delivered.

This facility is especially important to women who live where there are no doctors nearby. In such places in the developing world, a complication as common as the need for a cesarean section can cost a mother and child their lives.

Suzanne's life exemplifies two important lessons for me.

One is that when strong women are empowered and given choices, they can improve the quality of their lives, and the lives of their families and their communities. In fact, experts believe that the solution to some of the developing world's most pressing problems may lie in raising the station of women.

The other important lesson Suzanne's life illuminates is that whether a fellow human being lives across the street or across the world, his or her welfare should be a matter of concern to us.

One final tribute to Suzanne: I told Suzanne that despite all the teasing I'd taken over the years for calling her "the neighbor lady," if anyone ever came to me asking for a brief description of who she was, I would tell them that "Neighbor Lady to the World" said it best.

When the Benefits of
Neighboring Come Full Circle

*We all warm ourselves by fires we did not build and
drink water from wells we did not dig.*
—Robert Lawrence Smith

There is an unconscionable disparity—and egregious inequity—between the way that we live and the way the people of the developing world live.

There are also endless possibilities for helping these distant neighbors of ours improve the quality of their lives.

Here's an example.

Having been to Bangladesh, I can tell you that this morning a neighbor of ours there—a young mother—was making her way through the crowded capital city of Dhaka (a city of at least 400,000 rickshaws).

She was worried because the baby in her arms was dangerously dehydrated from diarrhea. Diarrhea has been one of the biggest killers of children around the globe, and Bangladesh has had one of the highest child mortality rates in the world.

Can we really impact such immense problems?

The answer is yes.

By tonight that mother in Dhaka—the one rushing her baby to the hospital—will most likely be at home in bed with her baby sound asleep beside her.

I saw dozens of mothers just like her at that hospital in Dhaka.

Thanks to some impressive science, international cooperation, and a process called oral rehydration, 95 percent of those babies leave the hospital just fine.

Doctors rehydrate these babies' intestines by giving them a solution to drink that consists of little more than water and salt and sugar. Every year that process spares millions of families the unspeakable pain of losing a child.

The International Center for Diarrheal Disease Research, Bangladesh, pioneered oral rehydration. Then a group called the Bangladesh Rural Advancement Committee took it out into the field to 13 million mothers. As a result, the infant death rate in Bangladesh has dropped dramatically.

It appears that soon there will be a vaccine available to protect children from the scourge of diarrhea.

All this shows that when we put our best minds to the task and work together, we can help our neighbors solve some seemingly impossible problems.

And it suggests that sometimes when we do this, unexpected blessings flow back our way.

I say that because the miracles worked by this simple life-saving solution didn't end in the world's poorest countries—and mothers and fathers everywhere should be celebrating that fact.

Today when babies in Los Angeles or London become dehydrated from diarrhea or the stomach flu, their parents are often told by the doctor to treat them with a similar electrolyte solution that happens to be available to them under brand names such as Pedialyte.

American moms and dads can buy it right off the shelves of their neighborhood supermarket—thanks in part to the same life-changing research that began in Bangladesh.

Portraits of Courage

*Courage is not simply one of the virtues but the form of
every virtue at its testing point.*

—C. S. Lewis

Anyone who believes that the poorest peoples of the
world don't treasure their children as much as we do ours
is simply wrong.

One of my most prized possessions is a photograph
of Nelson Mandela, Jimmy Carter, and me together at a
place called the Zola Clinic in South Africa. Each of us is
holding a baby in his arms.

It's a great picture. And I have always felt certain that
if it ever made its way into a newspaper the caption
would read: "Babysitting—Two Nobel Prize Winners and
a Retired Lawyer."

Pregnant women who were HIV positive were coming
to the Zola Clinic to be treated with a drug they knew
could drastically reduce their chances of transmitting the
virus to their unborn babies.

If you want to touch the hearts of grown men and remind them of the reasons they have taken on great challenges, hand them a child they've helped save. Bill Gates Sr. (left), Nelson Mandela (former president of South Africa), and Jimmy Carter (former president of the United States), at the Zola Clinic, Soweto, South Africa.

The mothers of the babies we were holding had come there for treatment during their pregnancies.

Tests done that day indicated that—thanks to four-dollar doses of the new drug—each of the babies we were holding in our arms was healthy and not infected with the virus.

As I held the little baby boy I had in my arms I marveled at the wonders of modern medicine. I marveled even more at his mother's courage.

Like all the other women present in that clinic that morning, she was well aware of the terrible stigma that befalls a woman in Africa who even comes forward to be tested for this disease. She knew she would become a pariah in her community.

But she had come forward, anyway, in the hope of saving her baby's life.

Some people seem to have a perception that women in poorer countries are ignorant about family planning and have children, one after another, without thought.

That perception tends to change when they realize how much courage it takes to have a baby in the developing world. It's estimated that more than 500,000 women and 4 million newborns die every year from the complications of pregnancy or childbirth.

Ask one of these women why they have another child, and you're likely to be told they do so in the hope of having one survive to adulthood.

Those living in poor communities don't have IRAs or savings accounts or social security. There may be only a tiny rice field in the retirement plan. They know that if they become too old to grow rice, or if they have an attack from malaria that keeps them from planting at the proper time they—and their loved ones—will starve.

Research over the past several decades has shown that when mothers begin to see that the children they have will survive, they tend to have fewer of them. Fewer and healthier children mean a better life for the whole family.

Many people argue that disease and poverty are economic issues or national security issues. But to me, these are humanitarian issues. We're talking about human beings who have infinite worth in their own right. People are dying, and we can save them; and that ought to be enough.

Africa, We See You

This land needs to help its men who will never let
themselves be discouraged.
—Albert Schweitzer

Whenever I visit Africa, I receive warm welcomes from the people there.

I remember once arriving in the Central African Republic where we were greeted with songs, drums, and marvelous dancing.

Then the music stopped, and I was called upon to offer some suitably dignified response. At such moments, I have often been thinking to myself something like: "Gee, I wish I could dance like that!"

Not long ago in Uganda, I could no longer resist the beat of the music and finally joined in on the dance.

On my first trip to Africa in 2001, I traveled to Mozambique to attend the first-ever vaccination day supported by an international group our foundation helped launch.

The first child in line for a vaccination was a little baby girl who had been through every imaginable hardship. But she had survived it all. And there she was—in her mother's arms—waiting for her vaccination.

Her name in Portuguese was Esperanza. Translated into English, Esperanza means "Hope."

On that first trip to Africa and on every one since, I've met or heard stories about people there whose lives express so much hope.

One of those people is a mother with two children. I picture her walking.

She is on a dirt trail, with one child in her arms and another at her side. She has just heard there is a vaccination day taking place twenty miles from where she lives. There is no bus to take. (There are few roads for that matter.) But she is determined to get her children vaccinations. So she is walking.

I can't tell you her name, but I know something of her heart. And I can put dozens of mothers' faces to her story.

I have met her all over the world because for every Esperanza, there is a mother or grandmother like her.

There's another mother who fills me with hope. And I picture her singing.

In Africa, good news and important messages are often passed on through song. This mother is part of a group of women who sing and dance before crowds of up to a thousand people at a time—singing a message to other mothers to tell them that if they get bed nets treated with insecticide for their children to sleep under they can protect them from the mosquitoes that transmit malaria.

One of my most hopeful images of all is that of a Ugandan seed grower I met. When I think of her, I picture her standing at a lectern at Harvard.

She has been there.

She was invited to speak at the Harvard Business School about the business model for the thriving concern through which she is breeding heartier disease-resistant seeds for Africa's future harvests. Beautiful, elegant, well spoken, she is a member of a new breed of female entrepreneurs who are developing Africa's vast potential while they improve their own fortunes.

One thing Africa is *not* is hopeless.

Africa is many countries and many cultures filled with spirited, resourceful people working hard to overcome their challenges. It may be important for their future for the rest of the world to acknowledge that we see that.

They say that in certain traditionally Zulu parts of South Africa, when two people greet each other the first one uses words that mean "I see you."

The other person answers with words that mean "I am here."

This reflects their belief that a person is not a person unless he or she is seen by others.

That greeting is a powerful statement about how much being recognized and encouraged by others in our lives has to do with the kind of people we become. It also drives home the role community plays in all our lives.

So as a citizen of a community that is now global I would like to say:

Africa, we see you.

Walking with Giants

One name that stands at the top of any list of the giants of philanthropy is "Rockefeller."

When I began reading about the Rockefellers I noticed that there were some unexpected little connections between our families.

The first one was that the person who helped John D. Rockefeller develop his approach to his philanthropy was a fellow named Gates.

Frederick Gates was not a relative of ours, but he placed a similarly high value on doing his homework. He consulted scores of experts and claimed to have read hundreds of books in putting together his ideas for the Rockefellers' philanthropy.

When I read of Frederick Gates's scholarship, Trey was beginning to devour anything he could get his hands on that had been written about the problems he and

Melinda hoped to address with their philanthropy. (He wasn't up to hundreds of books, yet.)

In my studies, I learned that it was John D. Rockefeller's son—John D., Jr.—who took over the task of giving away his father's money. And I wondered if I was the only dad in philanthropic history charged with giving away his son's money.

The Rockefellers have done so many things for so many people it's hard to get your arms around it.

Every corner we've turned in the field of global health, we've found that the Rockefellers were already there and had been there for years.

When we committed to childhood immunization we found ourselves building on efforts the Rockefeller Foundation had helped launch and fund in the 1980s.

When we became interested in fighting malaria and tuberculosis, we learned that the Rockefellers had been studying the prevention and treatment of such diseases around the globe for, in some cases, as long as a hundred years.

A similar dynamic held true in the case of HIV/AIDS.

A lesson we learned from studying and working with the Rockefellers is that to succeed in pursuing audacious goals you need like-minded partners with whom to collaborate.

And we learned that such goals are not prizes claimed

by the short-winded. The Rockefellers stay with tough problems for generations.

Nowhere is that truer than in the field of agriculture, where they've worked to increase agricultural production, feed a hungry world, and lift the poor out of poverty.

In the early twentieth century, when the U.S. rural South resembled a developing country, they supported the testing of new crops and sponsored movable schools where poor black farmers and their wives could learn everything from the most modern farming methods to how to preserve food through canning.

Between the 1940s and the 1960s the Rockefeller and Ford foundations, working with the governments of developing countries, transformed farming methods in Latin America and Asia. That work—later named the Green Revolution—doubled food production in the developing world, combating hunger and saving hundreds of millions of lives. In 1970, the Rockefeller Foundation scientist who pioneered that effort, Dr. Norman Borlaug, was awarded the Nobel Peace Prize.

Inspired by the Rockefeller Foundation's success, our foundation has joined with them to launch a new Green Revolution in Africa.

History suggests that no country of any size has been able to lift itself out of poverty without raising productivity in agriculture.

We expect that, over time, African farmers will be able to produce two or three times as much food as they are growing now and sell what they don't need.

All this should help tens of millions of people in sub-Saharan Africa lead more prosperous lives.

Reaching that audacious goal will involve everything from supporting the breeding of new, more resilient varieties of Africa's staple crops to developing financing options that encourage commercial banks to lend to farmers at affordable interest rates. It will entail creating new markets, turning the tide of subsistence farming, focusing on small farmers, and transforming African nations from net importers to net exporters.

We are identifying the people we think have the best chance of succeeding and helping them acquire the technology and knowledge they need.

People like Josephine, the Ugandan seed entrepreneur who went to Harvard to speak about the thriving wholesale seed business she started in her backyard.

Many businesses like Josephine's might not exist were it not for work done by the Rockefellers.

Some suggest that the Rockefeller's philanthropic tradition may trace all the way back to John D. Rockefeller's mother, Eliza Davidson Rockefeller, a devout woman who raised her children to be practicing Christians.

Well, I think Mrs. Rockefeller would have been thrilled

to meet Josephine as I did and know that values passed down through six generations of her children's children were helping women feed their families, improve their circumstances, and better their country's prospects.

In reading *The Story of the Rockefeller Foundation* by Raymond Fosdick—a history of the first fifty years of the Rockefellers' philanthropy—I found many stories worth sharing. But one in particular I will always remember.

In the 1940s two men who had lived in Germany and died in the Holocaust's death camps both left sizable amounts of money to the Rockefeller Foundation.

One was a doctor and the other was an industrialist.

They did not know one another. And they were unknown to the Foundation. One can only assume that in that dark time these two men looked upon the Rockefeller Foundation as the only organization worthy of their trust.

If many years from now the Bill & Melinda Gates Foundation inspires anywhere near that level of trust, we will know we've done our jobs.

The People You Meet
Showing Up

It is not so much their subjects the great teachers teach
as it is themselves.
—Frederick Buechner, *Listening to Your Life*

One of the rewards of showing up is that you meet the most amazing people.

A perfect example of such a person in my own life is Dr. Bill Foege.

He grew up poor in a small farm town in Eastern Washington.

As a young boy, inspired by the writings of Dr. Albert Schweitzer, he dreamed of becoming a doctor who would tend to people in Africa. That dream set him on a path that led to Nigeria, where he worked as a medical missionary and became the now world-famous epidemiologist who helped mastermind the eradication of smallpox.

Bill Foege has shown up as many things for many people.

His adventures around the globe read like a novel. As

the former director of the Centers for Disease Control, he focused attention on preventing and treating HIV/AIDS. As the instigator behind the Task Force on Child Survival he helped save the lives of millions of children. Dr. Foege has received some of medicine's highest honors, and was recently named one of "America's Best Leaders" by *U.S. News and World Report.*

During our foundation's earliest days, Dr. Foege helped us develop a strategy for our global health work, guiding us as we explored the possibility of getting involved with vaccines and immunization. He remains a trusted advisor.

For me personally, however, Bill Foege is, above all, a teacher.

Among other things, he has taught me more about the meaning of the word *neighbor.*

Our neighbors, he says, include the one million parents who every month lose a child they will grieve forever to a disease that could easily have been prevented. And he suggests that our neighbors include those who will be born two hundred years from now.

The latter notion isn't surprising coming from him because he seems as connected to people who lived two hundred years ago as he is to me when we're talking.

When he tells his stories of those from ages past you

can almost feel their presence—the presence of the British scientist Dr. Edward Jenner, who in the late seventeen hundreds drew lymph from a pustule on the hand of a milkmaid who had cowpox and used it to vaccinate a boy against smallpox; the presence of Louis Pasteur, who later suggested that the world honor Dr. Jenner by referring to immunizations thereafter as vaccinations; the presence of Thomas Jefferson, who managed to keep the virus used for the smallpox vaccine alive all the way across the Atlantic so he could vaccinate everyone in his household.

Given his achievements, Dr. Foege could have an ego a mile wide. Instead, a personal exchange with him is a real-life encounter with the virtue of humility.

Despite all the human suffering he's witnessed, he carries with him an optimism that can light up a room. He would say that is because even in the most difficult situations those in his vocation can see how much we can do to make things better.

One lesson I have learned from him is that if you sense that you have a particular mission in life, you probably ought to pursue it. You might not get rich, but you will get to keep your soul and you might even change the world.

Perhaps the most encouraging thing I've learned from knowing Bill Foege is that though it is more often celebrity than heroism that captures the sound bites, there are still real honest-to-goodness heroes in our midst.

Bill Foege taught me that lesson in the best way any teacher can—by being one.

A Master Citizen

Every time I am preparing to give a commencement address I go around for weeks asking myself and anyone else who will listen, "What's most important for the graduates to hear about what matters in life?"

Last graduation season I came up with three things. Family, friends, and public service—in that order.

Private life has its rewards but I think it's important—and makes one's life richer—to be a part of something larger.

I have had the privilege of observing some who are masters at the art of being good citizens. One is my longtime friend Dan Evans.

He's been a successful engineer, three-time governor of the state of Washington, United States senator, and a college president. Even today, after more than fifty years of public service, if a tough public issue arises and he believes he can help, he jumps into the fray like a "go to" player in the NBA who always wants the ball when things get tight.

I realized how central his desire for action is to his special brand of leadership the day, many years ago, when he and his wife, Nancy, were visiting us at our place on Hood Canal. They had joined us for the weekend. We had a pretty full schedule of activities planned. However, Saturday afternoon there was a short lull.

We were all sitting on our deck waiting for more guests we had invited to come for dinner. Dan got restless. Like a kid, he said, "Gee, isn't there anything to do around here?" I thought for a minute and then replied that we'd been intending to repaint the stripes on our pickleball* court.

Dan immediately responded: "Great. Where's the paint?"

I gave him the paint and he spent the afternoon on the job.

One thing I learned from observing Dan over the

---

*For those unfamiliar with the great sport of pickleball, it's a family sport played on a court about the size of a badminton court.

years has become part of my definition of a good citizen. That is: a good citizen is a person who is always looking for something to do.

Dan's life embodies the qualities that elicit respect from others.

He championed environmental issues when doing so wasn't yet popular. He worked tirelessly for a more equitable state tax structure when that wasn't popular either. He won debates and lost debates.

But even those who disagreed with him never questioned his integrity.

I'll never forget the expression of respect that occurred during the opening ceremonies for the Kingdome sports arena in Seattle. Dan had announced shortly before this that he wasn't going to run for governor again, and when he and Nancy were introduced, the entire audience of some sixty thousand people, who had been relatively quiet until that moment, stood and offered a thunderous burst of applause that lasted for a long time.

People were cheering for his honesty and his extraordinary performance throughout a long and distinguished career in public service. He always did what he thought was right, regardless of political pressure.

In my mind he stands as a shining example for both politicians and for the people who elect them.

I once thought I needed to write an essay to leave behind for my children on how crucial it is to always do the right thing.

Then I remembered that they grew up around Dan Evans.

There's No Problem Bigger
Than We Are

Many people imagine Rotary Clubs as places where businesspeople meet once a week to sell each other their products.

Well, I had never been to as many Rotary meetings as I have since we started our foundation. That's because one cannot be passionate about immunizing the world's children without coming to *revere* Rotary.

More than twenty years ago, when most volunteer efforts were aimed at solving problems that existed down the street, Rotary took on a global fight nobody believed they could win. A fight to end polio worldwide.

Since then Rotary has revolutionized our thinking about the possibilities that exist for ordinary people to significantly change the world.

Talk about fighting polio doesn't stir every soul in

America anymore because it no longer is a serious threat here. But this wasn't always so.

My daughter Kristi was born in 1953. At that time, there were major polio epidemics in this country. No vaccine was yet available. Like so many other parents, I worried that if she wandered into the wrong swimming pool my little girl could contract polio and end up in an iron lung.

Mass immunization campaigns in the 1950s and 1960s ended such fears for most American parents. By the 1980s nobody cared about polio. Nobody, that is, but Rotary.

At that time polio was still paralyzing a thousand children a day in poorer countries. That's why in 1985 more than a million Rotarians from roughly 140 countries—and every Rotary Club in the world—took on the challenge of creating a polio-free world.

What they have accomplished since then defies description. Worldwide, cases of polio have declined by 99 percent.

Rotary members have done everything from spending their vacations immunizing children in faraway places, to lobbying heads of state, to negotiating cease-fires in civil wars long enough to get millions of children vaccinated.

They've shown us how to mobilize people, raise more money than anybody thought volunteers could, and create private-public partnerships that can take on large-scale global problems.

I believe–as do most experts–that Rotary will achieve its audacious goal of eradicating global polio.

Along the way they have taught us that when we are inspired to work together in the interest of an engaging cause, there is no problem bigger than we are.

These Numbers Are
Our Neighbors

About suffering they were never wrong,
The Old Masters: how well they understood
Its human position; how it takes place
While someone else is eating or opening a window
or just walking dully along . . .
—W. H. Auden

An epidemiologist friend of mine, Dr. Sally Stansfield, once told a story that goes a long way toward explaining the blind spot people sometimes have about the suffering of others.

She had accompanied her then eleven-year-old son to a funeral for a classmate who had committed suicide.

After the service her son said to her, "I wish this had happened to someone I didn't know."

That's how we sometimes feel about the loss of a child on the other side of the world. We want to protect ourselves from the pain of knowing how truly tragic it is.

It may be natural to turn away, but if we do, the

hope that sometimes resides next to the pain may escape us.

Look at these numbers and you may be able to feel a sense of hope about what might be done to change them.

- Even in developed countries, the poor die five to ten years before the rich.
- In the last twenty-five years, the number of people in Sub-Saharan Africa living on less than a dollar a day has almost doubled.
- Every thirty seconds a child somewhere in the world dies of malaria.

The hope that resides beside that last statistic is this: Some scientists are now working on a malaria vaccine to prevent the disease, while others are investigating better treatments for those who already have it.

I know we can change these numbers. In fact, I've seen dedicated people all over the world changing them.

We can and will conquer these problems when, instead of turning away, we learn to embrace them as our own.

Public Will

Time and time again I've seen optimism triumph over pessimism.

During the Great Depression of the thirties you didn't have to be a pessimist to worry about the American dream of a better life ahead. But what we learned from those grim times is that the human spirit is resilient and that optimism and hope can trump pessimism.

After World War II the GI Bill paid for my college education, along with that of thousands of other returning soldiers. Not everyone supported the GI Bill; people were afraid that the nation couldn't afford it, and that sending ordinary Americans to college would somehow reduce the academic rigor of our universities.

History proved them wrong on all counts: Our universities were invigorated by the influx of fresh and eager minds, and growth in the nation's tax revenues, stimulated by the higher incomes of an educated citizenry, exceeded many times over the amount Americans invested in themselves through the GI Bill.

Soon after the end of World War II, the United States initiated what was called the Marshall Plan, an unprecedented program that invested many millions of dollars to help our allies—and our former enemies—recover from the ravages of war. The Marshall Plan is regarded as a monumental act of goodwill now, but was not universally supported at first because it was costly. The benefits from the quicker economic recovery of Europe, and the subsequent growth in world trade, far exceeded the cost. And, perhaps even more important, the United States was recognized everywhere as a strong and generous nation.

Later on, I lived through the years of what history now calls the Cold War—through the Berlin Blockade, through the Cuban Missile Crisis, through decades of saber rattling. A third world war seemed so certain to Americans that some built backyard bomb shelters; children learned to "duck and cover" in school in the event of an atom-bomb attack; people were so afraid of a Communist plot on our shores that politicians, actors, teachers, and many others were blacklisted as Communist sympathizers. The free world triumphed in that long Cold War through the force of its ideals and values.

And one of the greatest triumphs I've seen in a life-time is the civil rights movement, which continues today. Courageous men and women talked, and marched, and died in the cause of equal justice. The work they began is not yet complete, but their example has illuminated for all of us the endless possibilities of a society that offers all its people equal rights, equal justice, and equal opportunity.

My optimism for global progress is based on people and places I've seen around the world.

In my travels for the Bill & Melinda Gates Foundation I've met many people who are, in fact, changing the world—doctors and nurses who have taken leave from practices in the developed world to bring health and hope to impoverished areas.

I've met physicians who were born in poorer countries, studied and earned their degrees in the United States, and went back home to make a difference there.

Over the years I've met legions of good people, including numerous representatives of other foundations, at work every day under difficult circumstances to reduce and eliminate poverty, to improve health, to enhance women's rights, to secure land rights for farm families, to feed the hungry.

In recent years, the work of all of those individuals and organizations has encouraged a sense of global responsibility. In September of 2000 some 147 heads of state and government gathered at the United Nations to express their determination to end extreme poverty, disease, and environmental degradation. They expressed their hope that new technologies, heightened global awareness, and increasing wealth could be applied to solve problems, and they agreed on the eight Millennium Development Goals and on target dates for reaching them. The goals are designed to promote poverty reduction, improve education, advance maternal health and gender equality, and combat child mortality, HIV/AIDS, and other diseases.

The poorer countries among those represented at the Assembly pledged to govern better and to invest in their people through health care and education. Richer countries pledged to support them through aid, debt relief, and fairer trade. For the United States, and for other developed countries, the pledge is 0.7 percent of our gross domestic product to further the Millennium Development Goals.

Pessimists take note: Who among us during the dreary years of the Great Depression, or the frightening times of the Cold War, or the most difficult days of the civil rights movement would have bet big money that 147 nations from around the world would convene, deliberate, and then endorse a set of international development goals and set a timetable for reaching them?

I've thought a lot about historical tipping points such as this—how events and cultures and ideas combine at just the right moment to create change.

In a democracy, and in an increasingly democratic world, I believe that the tipping force for change is something called public will. It's an abstract concept, one you can't touch, or photograph, or buy at the store.

But when important things happen, it's because the public had the will to make them happen. And when nothing happens, it's because the public isn't willing. Public will is the reason why the civil rights movement happened in the 1960s, but not in the 1940s.

Public will is the sum total of every person's individual, deliberate acts of citizenship. You join a club. You read a newspaper. You sign a petition. You write a letter. You vote. You make a contribution. You have a friendly argument. If those clubs and newspapers and petitions and letters and votes and contributions and arguments predominantly point in the same direction, *that's* public will.

Public will is manifest when the right thing to do becomes consensus and people generally start expressing the convictions they share in everything they do.

That's precisely what I think happened when representatives of all those nations convened to formulate the Millennium Development Goals. They did so because global public will has evolved to support such goals.

The generation that is just now taking its place in the world is increasingly aware of global events. My hope is that they will take on the cause of global equity as their challenge the way our generation took on civil rights.

Let me tell you why I believe they will.

Eight years after those countries got together and created the Millennium Development Goals a granddaughter of mine came home from school with an assignment that amazed and delighted me.

Her homework was to learn about the Millennium Development Goals.

How a Hole in the
Fence Led a Boy from
Poverty to Poetry

That exchange brought home to me for the first time a
precious idea: that all humanity is somehow together.
—Pablo Neruda

I remember being taken with something the Nobel Prize-winning poet Pablo Neruda wrote about the power of being a good neighbor.

According to Lewis Hyde, author of *The Gift: Imagination and the Erotic Life of Property*, Neruda said that one day when he was a little boy growing up in southern Chile he was playing in a lot behind his house, peering through a hole in a fence.

Then, sensing something was going to happen, he pulled back.

At that moment he saw something come through that hole in the fence. It was the hand of a boy his age.

A moment later the hand was gone. But in its place

was a gift. A small well-worn toy sheep Neruda found magical.

His response was to take the sheep and then go and get a treasure of his own—and place it in the hole in the fence, in exchange.

Years later, he wrote of that exchange. He said:

To feel the love of people whom we love is a fire that feeds our life. But to feel the affection that comes from those whom we do not know . . . is something still greater and more beautiful because it widens out the boundaries of our being and unites all living things.

Neruda went so far as to hint that his poetry might have been his gift back to the world in response to that one moment of intimate human connection shared with a boy whom he would never meet.

It's hard to even imagine the extent of the gifts our neighbors in the developing world may one day return to the world at large if we're able to address the unconscionable disparity and egregious inequity that exist between the way that they live and the way that we live.

A Place to Start

The late Dr. Lewis Thomas, scientist, author, and former head of Memorial Sloan-Kettering Cancer Center, wrote

One of the nicest things about representing a major foundation is that you meet the best people. Here I am with a few of them in Delhi, India.

eloquently about the evidence of cooperation and collaboration found in most earthly life forms, including us.

He suggests that collaboration is fundamental to life and progress, and I couldn't agree with him more.

I have witnessed the power of collaboration, in many different forms, and with no small degree of awe, in many parts of the world.

I suspect the famous anthropologist Margaret Mead had the same experience before writing words now renowned among those who volunteer for good causes: "Never doubt that a small group of thoughtful, committed citizens can change the world. Indeed, it is the only thing that ever has."

I also believe whether it is in our roles as spouses or parents, family members or friends, citizens or simply human beings . . . everything begins with showing up.

A remarkable friend of mine was married to an equally remarkable man who died prematurely as the result of a devastating illness.

At the end of her first year of being alone, she sent her friends a Christmas letter that was newsy and positive and said, though not in so many words, that she was doing okay.

In closing that letter she shared something she had

read in *Kitchen Table Wisdom* by Dr. Rachel Naomi Remen that she found inspiring and challenging.

The words she sent me coincide directly with what I believe.

> *Life is the ultimate teacher, but it is usually through experience and not scientific research that we discover its deeper lessons. We are all here for a single purpose: to grow in wisdom and learn to love. We can do this through losing as well as through winning, by having and by not having, by succeeding or by failing. All we need to do is to show up openhearted for class . . . So fulfilling life's purpose may depend more on how we play than what we are dealt. You have to be present to win.*

The message, perhaps?
It all begins with showing up.

ACKNOWLEDGMENTS

In addition to the people you'll meet in these pages, there are others who helped make this book possible, but whose stories are not told here. On that account, I'd like to extend thanks and gratitude to the friends and co-workers who helped me find just the right pictures among boxes of family photographs; who checked dates, facts, and references from old documents; and who questioned easy assumptions with hard questions. Thanks, then, to my longest-tenured assistant and long-time friend of our family, Bonnie Clanin, and to Lynn Culp, Erica MacDonald, Ryan Rippel, Jeremy Derfner, Jennifer Masters, and Jeannette Yim.

And thanks to Jim Braman who kept alive stories about the people and events that touched our lives in the 1930s. Jim is an engaging storyteller, and someone I've had the honor to call "friend" these last seventy-five years.

And thanks to Monica Harrington, a communications expert who was a champion of this book before it became one, and who has the experience and skill to help introduce the finished work to readers.

Thanks to Mary Ann Mackin who helped me envision a book for a broader audience while I was writing one first intended only for my children, and who helped craft a coherent whole from hundreds of individual stories. And also to Tom McCarthy for his editorial support.

Thanks to Andrew Wylie and Scott Moyers, both of the Wylie Agency, who read a scant dozen pages or so and, on the basis of that glimpse, were able to imagine the next two hundred. And thanks to Roger Scholl, a Doubleday Publishing Group senior editor charged with turning a manuscript into a book.

And, finally, and most important of all, continuous thanks and gratitude to my family for their support and encouragement. To my wife, Mimi, and to my children, Kristi, Trey, and Libby, who reviewed drafts and offered suggestions in matters where my memory had not served me well enough.

Thanks to all of you for showing up.

INDEX